CHRYSALIS:

The Transformation
of the
Human Soul

EMILEE J. KERN

This is a work of non-fiction. Some names have been omitted to protect the privacy of the individuals. All stories in this book are my personal recollection of the events.

Cover art by Jessica Millman Tattoos
Cover design by Sweet 15 Designs
Editing and interior design by Grammar Goddess Editing
Editorial advice by Sylvana C. Candela

ISBN: 978-0-578-89357-0

To my mother and my daughter.
You both are an inspiration for my healing.
May the work that I have done on myself
have influence on the both of you.

Contents

Introduction

"Manifest, but also do the work." ~ Unknown

IF THIS BOOK has found its way into your hands, then you are likely someone who is on the verge of learning how to manifest the life they desire or actively using manifestation techniques but looking for more inspiration. Wherever you are in your journey with manifestation, I am optimistic that my stories will provide you motivation to help you on your way.

I've written this book to share the stories of how a young woman from Wisconsin, who only knew life as it was taught to her, took a giant leap of faith and co-created a life she couldn't have imagined for herself just 10 years ago.

I will take you through my beginning, explain what I consider my "spiritual awakening," and how I actively used visualization tools to shift my life into the direction I wanted. My stories include putting an end to hurtful relationship patterns, aligning myself with my core values and passions, connecting to my purpose, pregnancy loss, and finding love.

This is not a story about luck, although I do believe in Karma and a touch of fate. This is a story of doing the work through self-realization, mindset reboot, acknowledging hurtful patterns, learning lessons, and healing trauma in combination with affirmations, visualizations, and manifestation techniques. Heartbreak still finds its way into our lives regardless of how magical we are; as long as we are alive on this planet, there are lessons for us to learn.

My friends who have witnessed my manifestations firsthand call me the "Queen of Manifestation." Although I would righteously own the title of a Queen, I do not wish to separate myself or claim to be more powerful than another. This magic is available to everyone equally. My wish is that by sharing my stories and the steps I've learned to utilize while manifesting, you will be able to create the life you have wished for. You are a Monarch Manifestor, be the Queen/King of your fruiting reality.

I will be taking you back to your child-like state of wonder and awe where you'll learn to truly feel and express gratitude while trusting that your needs are - and will always be - met. This will not come without effort. I will encourage you to take a good look at yourself, your thoughts, patterns, and even some of your trauma that keep you where you are today. We are going to take a holistic approach to healing, taking an honest look at which areas of your life are flourishing and which areas could use some improvement.

I will be guiding you through mindfulness meditations, affirmation exercises, and visualization techniques, all harmonizing with my own stories to inspire a shift in your consciousness. I wish to inspire hope and belief in you so that all of your biggest dreams come true.

By the end of this book you will have an understanding of how visualization works and how to use the tools provided to attract the life you desire.

We will also be creating a Vision Board at the end of the book. A Vision Board is a collage of images used as a visual representation of your goals and desires.

I want my readers to know that you ARE worthy. You ARE powerful. You are a Monarch Manifestor, and I am excited for your journey to unfold.

Chapter 1 – The Ruins of the Sugar-Cube Castle

"As traumatized children we always dreamed that someone would come and save us. We never dreamed that it would, in fact, be ourselves, as adults." ~ Alice Little

I WAS 12 YEARS OLD when the last bit of childlike awe and wonder left my body. My parents were getting a divorce, and no matter how much I prayed, I could not keep them together. I was not raised religious, but each night I would pray, "Now I lay me down to sleep," and beg, "Please God, do not let my parents get a divorce."

My heart can still feel the pain this caused, and the barrier to protect my heart from future hurt is still in place. It remembers exactly when and why I gave up believing in something of a higher power. God had not listened to me, therefore did not exist. That was my accusation and what I truly believed for the following 12 years.

Growing up in Wisconsin in a town populated with 60,000 people, bordered by cornfields, deemed it fitting that the high school I attended was nicknamed, "Cow Pie High."

I remember watching a group of denim- and plaid-clad "corn-fed boys'' turn an old Honda CRX on its side because a new student regretfully parked in the "farmer's row." These parking spots were reserved for big Ford and Chevy Pickup Trucks. This was not a place for the new city boy to park his foreign car. We lived in a GM town, after all. These same corn-fed boys would cruise the main strip on Friday evenings, burning through gas and blowing exhaust, while hollering at the girls all night. Races would be secretly arranged on the side streets, foreign and American cars alike.

High school was an interesting experience for me. Looking at my hometown today and seeing the same groups of friends together on social media, just as if it was a Friday night and they were gathering in the bleachers to cheer on their high school team at the football game or their annual spring break trip to Gulf Shores, makes me cringe.

Perhaps I feel envious because I was never part of a big friendship group like that, or because my mother being a foster mom my entire life with revolving kids coming and going influenced me to change my friends like I do my underwear. A probable combination of it all. After many years away from my hometown, lots of time spent in self-observation and therapy, I can now recognize my relationship patterns and where in my childhood they stem from.

At the time of my parents' divorce, I was in sixth grade. On top of my belief in something greater and the foundation in my home crumbling, I began to experience the reality of mean teenagers.

Two significant moments happened to me in middle school that set the tone of my character for the remainder of my adolescence until my later shift in consciousness.

The first one was the destruction of my sugar-cube castle. Every sixth grader in that school had to build a miniature castle from sugar cubes. I remember the delighted feeling of carrying mine home after I received my final grade. My mom had helped me complete the castle, she cut up a grass mat that came with my Little Tikes playhouse, and placed some of my toy figurines around the royal grounds. I proudly carried my castle like a trophy down the great steps and out the front door of the school. It was after three o'clock, and all of the students were rushing out of the front door towards their freedom. Three feet out of the door I felt an unfriendly shove from my right; an older teenage boy had intentionally knocked the castle out of my hands. It hit the cement ground and collapsed into a sugary ruin. Tears welled in my eyes as I hurried to pick up the scattered pieces of my masterpiece. Hair fell over my face as hurried feet passed by me. Some students smirked and made jokes as they saw the crisis, and some paused to help. I was as shattered as my castle while I carried the catastrophe on my 3-block walk home.

The second influential moment was just another typical day in middle school. During lunch break, I was interrogated by a trio of older girls. These girls were popular and rather intimidating. It was unspecified why they were interested in me or whether they even knew who I was.

"Why do you dress like that? We know you're not poor. You dress like a scrub," the leader of the group mocked.

The other girls laughed as their hierarchy spoke, condemning Emilee Nicholson unsatisfactory to their kind.

Thinking about it now, perhaps it was a compliment or a call to make a change in myself and the friends I had chosen. I was a 12-year-old seemingly normal girl who would have fit in with the popular kids who played sports and dressed "preppy," but the damage from home left me feeling dark inside. I wore baggy shirts adorned with controversial musicians, JNCO jeans – pants with leg openings of 30 inches or more, shaved the underneath of my hair, and pierced my own nose. My childhood room – once filled with Trolls and stuffed toys – had been overtaken by black lights and psychedelic fuzzy posters.

For the remainder of my school days until I graduated high school, I would keep myself distant from becoming part of any popular friendship groups. Aesthetically I would have fit in, but internally I did not belong.

Having my foundation crumble and experiencing bullying made me gloomy and my sadness turned into anger. Not knowing how to help me, my parents put me into counseling and the counselor prescribed antidepressants. Over the next years, my disconnect from myself and my anger towards others grew. Being volatile, aggressive and promiscuous at a young age acquired me an undesirable reputation. I would physically fight anyone who looked at me wrong and confront anyone who said anything about myself or my friends. Remembering how it felt when those girls first confronted me, I was determined that neither I nor anyone I cared for ever felt that way again. My actions caused more harm than I prevented.

That undesirable reputation followed me throughout high school and into my early twenties. Dependent on antidepressants, blacking out on alcohol, getting into bar fights, and sleeping around left me feeling lost. I felt unworthy of love, insecure, and had minimal self-respect. My validation came from strange men and lasted briefly. When I found myself in a relationship with a man, it was a swift fall into love, which spiraled down into control and mistrust, and always ended in some form of domestic violence.

Each relationship was the same as the last. I told them I loved them and morphed into a version of myself that fit them until we became one. My unrest would soon emerge, and I would begin to separate myself from the unit to be met with narcissism, anger, and abuse. I was not innocent nor a victim, I actively created these scenarios and was equally aggressive with some of the men. It wasn't until I recognized my pattern and sought the help I needed from my family that I was able to break away from this relationship pattern all together. That would be the first step in my awakening.

Chapter 2 – It's Time to Jump

"When you have come to the edge of all the light you have known and are about to drop off into the darkness of the unknown, faith is knowing one of two things will happen: There will be something solid to stand on or you will be taught to fly." ~ Richard Bach

YOU MAY HAVE HEARD the term "Spiritual Awakening;" that is the way I would label the beginning of my journey. A shift in consciousness that happened through self-realization and a change in my perspective.

It began during my last long-term relationship in Wisconsin. This would be the turning point in my pattern of abusive relationships. After months of shouting and shoving, I was finished with the relationship. We lived in a one-bedroom apartment, tucked away behind a golf course, surrounded by a dense forest. He was from out of town, I met him while he was working on the oil pipeline. He, being from out of town and not knowing my reputation, was appealing to me. He was a shiny new experience, and I couldn't have been more thrilled to get to know him. Although he was a new person from a different town, we quickly fell into the same patterns as my last few boyfriends.

We immediately fell in love, and I was quick to hide myself away from my friends and family to spend all of my time with him. After a few months together, I grew unhappy and began pulling away from him. He attempted to control me in response. The arguing began, and the slamming of doors became the smashing of fists and broken items throughout the home. This intensified to shoving and slapping, and we both had black eyes at one point in the relationship.

I worked down the road from our apartment as a cocktail waitress. There were times that I would have to cover scratches on his face with my foundation so he could come in and watch football. We lied about what happened and it made me sick to my stomach. The idea that my coworkers would know what we did to each other haunted me. It was probably obvious, and I am sure that speculative chatter went on outside of my presence. I lied to my family when they asked why I had a black eye, but they knew the truth. After years of watching my explosive behavior and having near-mental breakdowns, they knew how I could be.

Since the day the counselor prescribed me antidepressants, their first question to me was, "Did you take your pill?"

Whenever I had a violent episode or a fit of anger, they assumed I had skipped my daily dose of antidepressants. There wasn't a way out of this darkness. When I asked my doctor about my future with antidepressants, he told me I was probably one of the 40 percent of people who would need them for life. I believed it.

This destructive behavior, humiliation for my angry outbursts, and requirement to be medicated became my identity. I would never be anyone better than Emilee Nicholson, the girl with the reputation of getting drunk, fighting with women, and abusing her boyfriend. I despised myself and felt that I was full of darkness and unpleasantness.

This all began to transform with a change in my perception of myself. I remember the exact moment it began.

It was my 23rd birthday; my boyfriend and I went to the Wisconsin Dells for the night to celebrate. We rented a hotel room at the Great Wolf Lodge, a hotel with an indoor water park. The Wisconsin Dells is a tourist attraction town filled with waterslides, go-carts, and other draws for thrill seekers. The day before my birthday, an argument turned into a physical eruption, and I was feeling repulsed both with myself and him that day. I resented this man and knew I needed to get away. While exploring the Dells, we chose to ride on a giant slingshot that catapults you high into the sky on two bungee cords. We opted to purchase the DVD video recording of the experience.

My life changed when I watched the playback. I had never seen myself on video before that, and selfies were not quite a thing in 2010. Aside from glancing at myself in the mirror to do my hair and makeup, I did not know how I really appeared on the outside. It was my belief that with just one glimpse of me you would know the things I had done that made me unworthy of respect and love. I assumed the darkness I felt inside was evident on the outside.

Still feeling remorseful from the evening before, I watched the video and to my surprise, I didn't look angry, destructive, or unapproachable. There was a light emanating from me that I had never known before. I appeared kind and loveable. The very characteristics I admired in my two older sisters also existed within me. A spark of joy radiated from my heart as I witnessed my true essence. I was kind, loving, and gentle. The darkness I felt, and the person associated with it, was not my truth. For so long I had ached to be seen differently than the darkness I felt inside; I did not expect that it would be up to me to see it.

This was the first step towards a very long and on-going journey with self-love.

Days later, returning home to our apartment after my waitressing shift, I was greeted by a very green and foreign grasshopper. I had never seen one like this before, or at least I had never taken the time to observe a creature like it before. A peculiar knot formed in my stomach which I ignored and proceeded inside. Hours later, I noticed the hopper still perched outside on the tall glass window. The knot remained in my stomach as I peered a little closer. "It has something to tell me," I thought, as I moved as close as I could to observe it.

Noticing every detail on its body and appreciating its willingness to stay put while I invaded its personal space I heard, "It's time to jump."

The words came from inside myself, and I felt deep within the core of my being that the relationship I was in was over; this wasn't me anymore. I knew that I could change my circumstances and it was time to do so. This was my very first recollection of my intuition.

In the weeks that followed I stopped participating in the abuse and readied my escape. At first my family did not take me seriously because they did not witness my changes. Then, during one night of his violent episodes, I escaped to my mother's house to sleep on her couch. I woke up horrified to find him standing over me, anger blazing in his eyes. My mom woke up from the commotion and told him to leave. The anger grew as he was not able to physically hurt me in front of her, so he spit in my face and ripped a mirror off my car as his vengeance.

I was so grateful this happened because my mom knew that I needed immediate help. I was able to end the relationship with the aid of my family, they helped me pack my belongings and move into my grandmother's basement. It was in this basement that more realization and awakening would unfold.

Continuing to work at the restaurant, I flourished as a waitress and bartender. Staying single for the next several months helped me to see the patterns of my past relationships and focus on recreating who I had been over the last 12 or so years.

A coworker of mine was heavily influential on my journey as I was infatuated with her "vegan" lifestyle. Her way of living and raising her family roused every cell in my body. The concept of not eating meat and dairy was entirely new to me. She never tried to force her lifestyle on me, and openly answered every one of my questions.

A trip to the public library later, I had a stack of vegan-influenced titles to further my research. I quickly learned about the harm we do to ourselves, the animals, and the planet with our Standard American Diet (S.A.D.). I had never felt so much passion boil up inside of me before. This was it! My purpose! I was going to be VEGAN, and share it with the world. I began teaching myself how to prepare plant-based meals, and it was the most exciting thing I had ever done to that point. I felt alive and full of purpose. For the first time I felt like I was a good person. I felt like I was contributing to something important, and I was taking care of my body.

My lifestyle choices had an influence on my dating life. Trying to eat vegan at restaurants in 2011 was challenging. My lifestyle helped weed out potential boyfriends as my dates watched me eat my vegan food, unamused and uninterested in making a similar change. The choices helped me stand in my power, assert what I wanted for myself, and to choose myself each time. I would simply not fall into any relationship that would compromise who I was becoming, and I wouldn't be morphing into another human for the sake of being "loved."

Around this same time, I discovered Yoga. Focusing on my breathing, observing my mind, and laying in the stillness of *savasana* connected me more to my physical body. Yoga inspired a calmness within me, and I felt a sense of gratitude in my daily life. I would smile often at strangers and think more positively. I naturally began to practice nonjudgement and was more accepting of other people. With all of the changes I had made for myself and practicing Yoga, I was able to eliminate the need for antidepressants. The influence Yoga had on my life has inspired me to continue practicing and complete several hundred hours of Yoga Teacher Trainings. Yoga continues to be a big part of my life and mindfulness practice today.

While all of this change was happening within me, I received a suggestion from a friend to watch a movie titled *The Secret,* about the Law of Attraction. I located the DVD at the Metaphysical shop, and unknowingly was about to learn the most fascinating piece of information that would change my entire life. Immediately, I understood how my thoughts created my experience, and that I could manifest anything I desired through the practice of visualization. While watching the film, I visualized myself in my new dream car, which came to fruition within weeks. An opportunity to move to Hawai'i also materialized, and I moved there without hesitation, and am still here nearly a decade later.

By becoming aware of myself, beginning to practice self-love, finding my passions, feeling a true sense of gratitude, and following my purpose, I completely changed my life around.

Throughout the next chapters I will break this process down into realistic steps and stories from my experience.

Chapter 3 – Where Are You Now?

"You do not just wake up and become a butterfly. Growth is a process." ~ Rupi Kaur

IN THIS CHAPTER we are going to take a look at where you currently are in your life. Using a guided meditation followed by an exercise to examine the areas of your life and where you would like to see improvement will help you get a clear picture of what it is you would like to manifest.

I recommend recording yourself reading through the meditation on your voice memos app on your phone and listen back with headphones. You may also read through each subject and take a few minutes to contemplate the suggestions or have a partner read this to you. Take brief pauses between the questions to allow yourself time to reflect and answer.

Guided Meditation

Start by finding a comfortable seat or lying down. Gently close your eyes or find a soft gaze as you bring awareness to your breath. Relax the muscles of your face and jaw and roll your shoulders down and away from your ears. Allow your breath to roll up from your belly to your chest like a wave filling the space around your heart and gently exhale all of the air completely out.

Continue to breathe like this as you release your arms and legs towards the floor. Imagine a ray of sun shining on your face; greet the warm light with a slight smile and relaxed eyelids.

Continue to breathe in towards your heart. I am going to walk you through several categories, and I want you to consider what you are currently happy with and what you could improve.

Starting with your health and body, tell yourself what you are most happy with. Is there a feature you love most?
- What about your body are you most grateful for?
- Are you grateful for your body's strength and ability to heal?
- Do you love your hair or the color of your eyes?

Breathe this love and gratitude into your heart space.

Now consider if there are any improvements you would like to see in your body. Take a few breaths, and without judgement, think of what you would like to see change or what you would like your body to be able to do.

Send yourself compassion by breathing through your heart and take a final breath of gratitude, thanking your body for all that it has done for you.

Begin to shift your awareness to your friends, family, and social life.
- What does this area look like for you?
- What do you love most about the people in your life?
- Do they bring you joy and offer excitement?
- Are they supportive and encouraging?

Think about the special people in your life and your social activities while breathing gratitude into your heart. Take a few breaths here.

Now consider where you would benefit from a shift in these relationships and social circles you are part of.
- Is there anyone or anything that does not serve your highest good?
- Is anyone or anything holding you back or pulling you down?
- Are you wanting to attract new people and social opportunities into your life?

Bring your awareness to your breath, and breathe gratitude for the people in your life.

Checking in with your body, relax the space between your eyebrows and feel an imaginary hand wipe the frown lines away from your forehead.

Now consider your significant other. If they are in the picture, think about the attributes you love most about them. Feel the physical support they offer you and every way they lift you up. If you are not with someone and are searching, you can use your imagination to visualize what you would like to attract in your ideal partner.

Spend some time considering all the things about them that make you happy. Feel the gratitude for this person and allow love to radiate from the center of your heart. Take another breath, and then consider where your relationship could benefit from improvement.

If you are single, consider the ways past relationships could have been better and what it will look like next time you are in a relationship.

Send compassion to yourself and your partner/partner-to-be and say, "Thank you for loving and supporting me."

Let's move on to your spirituality. What beliefs do you hold and how have they benefited you?
- Do you practice a religion or connect to a higher power?
- If so, do you currently feel connected to this source of power?

- Are you feeling separate from your fellow human beings or any other part of the planet at this moment?

Take a few breaths to think about your belief system and how this brings benefit to your life and how connected to those beliefs you are in this moment.

Take a deep inhale through your nose and exhale through your mouth. Relax.

Let's move into your relationship with money and your career.
- What is your relationship like with money?
- Do you feel like your needs are met and you are provided for?
- Do you feel like you are lacking with the amount of money you need?

Breathe here and pay attention to any sensations in your body when you think about money.
- Do you grow tense in an area? Send your breath to the tension if it is there, and then relax.
- Think about your current career. Is your career in alignment with who you are?
- Does your career bring you joy?
- Does the amount of money you earn satisfy you?

Consider the amount of money you would need for you to feel satisfied if you are not currently happy with your finances.

Contemplate where you could improve in your career whether through a complete change, a position change, or promotion.

Ask, what is best for you here?

Let's relax again and move onto your home environment.
- How happy do you feel in your current home?
- Do you love where you live?
- Do you feel safe in your home?
- Do you have the necessary space you need?
- Are you happy with all of the inhabitants that live in your home?
- Are your neighbors nice?

- Is your neighborhood quiet, if that is what you prefer?

Consider where you would like to see improvements in your home environment.

Now let's take a moment to think of a topic that has not been covered. Is there an important area in your life you would like to give gratitude, and perhaps look at improving?

Take a moment to consider it here.

After reviewing all of these areas of your life, reflect on your self-worth.
- Do you feel worthy to have what you have?
- Do you feel comfortable asking for more?
- Do you believe that you deserve to have all you desire?
- Do you believe that you are worth more and deserve to be loved unconditionally?

Be honest with yourself and send yourself compassion if you feel a lack of worth in any of these areas.

Breathe gratitude through your heart for everything you have, and that we have touched on.

Affirm that you are ready to be honest with yourself surrounding your desires and your needs, and acknowledge that you deserve to have everything you want.

Inhale through your nose, sending the breath through your heart and exhale with an open mouth; loudly sigh if you please.

Gently wiggle your fingers and toes and open your eyes.

Happiness Graph Exercise

Next, take a look at the graph provided below and fill it in based on where you are right now. The bottom of the chart being the least happy and the top being the happiest. You may color the column all the way in or you can place a dot where you decide and connect the dots from each column. Both options will create a bar graph, and a look into where you are flourishing and where you could benefit from improvement.

Health	Family / Friends	Partner	Spirituality	Money / Career	Home	Self-Worth	

Example Graph:

Health	Family / Friends	Partner	Spirituality	Money / Career	Home	Self- Worth	Adventure / Travel

Example Graph:

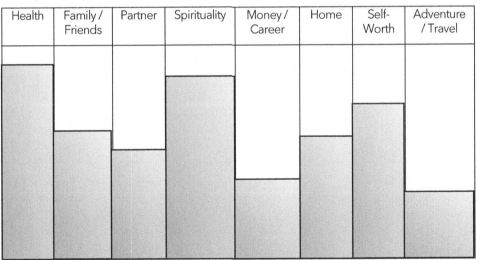

Health	Family / Friends	Partner	Spirituality	Money / Career	Home	Self- Worth	Adventure / Travel

Now that you have taken a look at your life, the areas where you feel the most happiness and also where you could improve, take some time to write out exactly what you desire in these areas. Begin to think about what it is you want to manifest for yourself in each of these areas. You will create your lists in Chapter 9.

Chapter 4 – Remember Who You Are

"Keep hanging out with yourself until you are you again." ~ Unknown

OUR CORE VALUES have been a part of our being since childhood, we might even suggest that we are born with them. When we take a look at the activities we enjoyed as a child, we may find that our passions developed then as well. Through a combination of conditioning, outside influence from family and friends, and trauma, it is possible that we have become disconnected from our true nature.

~ ~ ~

It is a Saturday morning, and eight-year-old Emilee is awake early. Her friends are still sleeping, exhausted from last night's roller skating and sleep over. Excitement is flowing through her as she anticipates a grand surprise for her friends; she is going to make them breakfast. She tip-toes up the basement steps into the kitchen of her family's ranch-style home. Quietly, she pulls out the milk, eggs, and bread for French toast and scrambled eggs. She quickly goes to work mixing the eggs with the milk, drenching the bread into the mixture, and frying up perfectly golden slices of French toast. The remainder of the mixture gets scrambled into eggs. Eloquently garnishing each plate with equal amounts of food, topping the toast with butter and syrup, Emilee ensures that everyone receives the exact presentation she imagines.

Not being concerned about disturbing her friends, this time Emilee bolts loudly down the stairs. She cannot contain her excitement as she impatiently wakes up her friends and hassles them to eat their breakfast. Half asleep and with tangled hair, her friends reluctantly walk up the stairs from the darkness of the basement to the intense morning light. Once adapted, the friends and Emilee all sit together and eat their breakfast. Forkfuls of delicious toast oozing maple syrup hit their mouths as they gush about all the fun they had the night before.

In this moment Emilee is pleased; she has provided nourishment for her friends by passionately preparing food.

In her early twenties, Emilee rediscovered her passion for cooking when she became vegan. She eagerly accepted the challenge to undo everything she had ever learned about the Standard American Diet, and taught herself how to prepare nourishing food without meat and dairy. Not having slumber parties as she did as a child, she took to social media to share her creations. Several of her friends were inspired by her passion and her recipes, and she began to co-host a vegan potluck evening with a friend. Collectively, each person would choose a plant-based recipe and bring it to share that evening. Everyone would gush over how impressed they were with the taste of a dish or their exploration with a new ingredient. It was bonding, inspirational, and the nourishment it provided ignited Emilee's passion. She loved fueling her inner fire by preparing the food and sharing it with others.

Passions and Core Values Exercise

This memory of wanting to cook and prepare meals for my friends is one of the most blissful memories of my childhood. In these reminiscences I was creative and tapping into my passions. I was doing something that came through the core of my being and made me happy; this was me accessing my true essence.

Later in life I was able to rediscover my passions through cooking for my friends. The same joy and excitement I experienced as a child filled me again. The desire to create nutritious meals for those I care about was something that has always existed within me.

Let's try an exercise to access your passions.

Think of a time in your childhood when you felt the most joyful. This could be a time you were actually creating something or participating in an activity. Perhaps you built a tree house, or you were in a ballet class.

I was the most joyful in my childhood when:

_____

because_____.

Our passions are what make us feel joyful, and the reasons these activities brought us joy are our core values. One of my core values is nourishment. I enjoyed preparing breakfast for my friends because I was providing them with nourishment.

We can compare this to our lives today by asking:

I am the most joyful when:

_____

because_____.

Today what brings you joy may be the same or perhaps it has shifted, but it is likely that the reasons these things bring you joy remain the same.

Complete these exercises with different activities that bring you joy and the reasons why. It may be something like "spending time with family," because I feel connected and supported. Connection and support would be two of your core values.

Your list can be as long as you would like, or you can shorten your list to a few words. Allow these values to be a deciding factor in choosing your community, your career, your beliefs, and activities. Stay connected to your personal power by staying connected to your core values, which are the true essence of your being.

Chapter 5 – The Price of Milk

"Life is hard for two reasons, you're either leaving your comfort zone or you're staying in it." ~ Unknown

WHILE WORKING HER SHIFT one afternoon at the restaurant, Emilee received a phone call from her father. He worked as a contractor near Chicago, and his job required him to travel constantly. He was her favorite person and she happily took a break to chat with him.

He said, "I am going to Hawai'i for my next job in a few months; I will be staying there for six months."

For the first time since the grasshopper, Emilee received an intuitive message, a moment of knowing. She affirmed, "I am moving to Hawai'i." Feeling more certain about it than anything she ever had decided, she felt the pull from somewhere deep inside of her.

"You can't move to Hawai'i," he countered.

"Why not?" she asked, staggered.

"Because you can't just quit your job."

The excitement and life drained from Emilee's body as she remembered you can't just do things like that. You don't just quit your job and take leaps of faith towards unseen places without knowing how much a carton of eggs and a gallon of milk cost, and how you will work to pay for them.

"You are right, Dad," she agreed, feeling defeated.

Months went by with Emilee working at her job, passionately cooking vegan food, practicing the Law of Attraction, and feeling the happiest she had ever been since her childhood. She practiced Yoga and loved "Power Pump" classes at the local gym where she was hired to become a personal trainer. She was still single and casually going on dates without falling in love and returning to old patterns for the first time in her life. Her passion for food and holistic wellness filled the void that once was her need for connection. She felt like a good human, she felt that people liked her and saw the good in her. Her patrons at the restaurant did not know of the old reputation she carried. They only knew of the happy, glowing girl making their Bloody Marys, and serving them fish fry on a Friday night. Her life had changed.

In April of that year, Emilee planned a trip to visit her dad on the island of O'ahu where he rented an ocean-front condo in Waikiki. Taking two and a half weeks off from work for her trip, because she would not just quit and move there without a plan, she headed out on the biggest adventure she would embark on up to that point.

While on the flight from ORD to LAX, she jotted down her goals for her visit on O'ahu. She would visit the Down to Earth Organic and Natural vegetarian grocery store. She would meet other vegans, and connect to the Vegetarian Society of Hawai'i. She was on a mission to meet like-minded people, as they were not abundant at that time in her small Wisconsin hometown.

During the layover at LAX, Emilee took a ritualistic shot of Jameson, and purchased a pack of fruity Mentos to enjoy during the flight. As she made her way to the gate a familiar symbol caught her eye. The Green Bay Packers logo stood out to her on a pair of men's board shorts. A tall, dark and quite handsome guy stood in line for the same flight as she. He was casually dressed in Green Bay Packers shorts, a beach tank and a baseball hat. His teeth were iridescently white as she observed him talking from a distance.

She is from Wisconsin, he likes the Packers. "I'm going to talk to him," she encouraged herself as she confidently walked over.

"Are you from Wisconsin?" she asked with a smile.

"No, I am from LA, but I love the Packers," he responded, seeming to be intrigued that a cute girl just randomly approached him at an airport.

They spoke until it was time to board the plane. During the conversation, she succeeded in getting his phone number; he was currently living in Waikiki and promised to show her around.

During the flight, Emilee struggled to find an appropriate snack that fit into her diet. "Why is there dairy in salsa?" she judgingly whispered, as the only close option was chips and salsa. The Mentos she had probably were not vegan either, but they would suffice for now.

Halfway through the flight she looked up to see that handsome guy in the Packer's shorts walking towards her carrying a hot fudge sundae as an offering. He was seated in a higher class and brought her the treat from his accommodations.

Absolutely thrilled, she took it in her hand and admired it in appreciation. The reminder of her choice to restrain from dairy broke her excitement as she handed it back and said, "I am vegan, I will not eat this."

His face dropped in embarrassment while neighboring passengers witnessed the amusing exchange.

"I will take a drink instead," she offered.

He smiled and quickly went to remedy his choice.

Emilee was proud of herself. By sticking to her passions and her values, she was still able to attract potential partners. She did not have to fall into old patterns with men; she was rewriting the way she would enter into relationships.

The first morning waking up in her dad's Waikiki apartment was extraordinary. The apartment had a giant window that overlooked the ocean and opened up almost like a balcony without the actual balcony. Daily rainbows could be seen on the horizon as well as turtles swimming below. It was a studio apartment and Emilee slept on a couch pushed right up to this marvelous window. Her father was working, so she was going to spend the day exploring on her own. A quick Facebook poll brought a recommendation from an old school mate who was a former Marine stationed on O'ahu, influencing her decision to venture to Duke's restaurant first. Duke's was a direct walk down the beach, and she left as early as possible to be there when it opened. Walking in the sand the entire way, she appreciated the views with Diamond Head crater to her right and the ocean to her left as she made her way to the restaurant.

She found a seat at the tiki bar and ordered a jalapeño margarita. She had never heard of such a drink, and at 10 in the morning, why not? It was afternoon back home, after all.

Enjoying her adventure and eager to make connections, she detected a young woman with long brown hair seated at the bar with her back turned towards Emilee. She was deep in conversation with the gentlemen she was with, but something about her laugh was very welcoming.

Emilee boldly tapped the woman on her shoulder, and the woman turned towards her. "Hi, I'm Emilee. Would you like to be my friend?"

A warm and laughter-filled conversation followed, and she discovered that her new friend had just moved here from Seattle and was renting an apartment with another girl she recently met on craigslist.

Over the next few days, Emilee spent time with the two women, and the three of them quickly became friends. They bonded over their shared adventures of moving away from home to an island in the Pacific. When she expressed her desire to live there, they offered her their couch as a place to sleep to get her started. She was also spending time with the guy from the airplane, and beginning to create a foundation for herself in just a few short days.

One afternoon over Mai Tais with her father, Emilee again expressed her desire to live in Hawai'i.

"Uh, you BELONG here," her dad asserted.

She knew what she had to do now. She was going to quit her job and move to Hawai'i. She flew back home after her trip and put in her two weeks' notice. She sold most of her belongings in a garage sale. She and her friends organized a Hawai'i-themed goodbye party, and she prepared for the biggest leap of faith she could take. Friends and family were curious and inspired by her choice, most of them confessing that they could never do something like that, although many of them wished they could.

With only a few hundred dollars to her name, she headed back to O'ahu to follow her passion and become part of a vegan community.

Emilee took a job at a trendy hotel as a pool server. Eventually, her father left the island, and she rented a room in a 5-bedroom house shared with college-aged girls. She bought a beach cruiser bicycle without gears, mainly for looks, and quickly regretted it during her hour-long bike rides home up the mountain after her long waitressing shifts. Many days she would spend half of her wages on cab fare home because she was just too exhausted and did not want to ride home in the dark.

With her passion still being her driving factor, her life was not exactly as she had hoped for several months after moving to Hawai'i. Still eating plant-based, having few options in the hotel cafeteria and making no connections with like-minded people, she tuned into her gut feelings and knew there was something else she must do. She felt it was her purpose to cook vegan meals and educate people on holistic wellness. She missed cooking the meals and still longed to be part of that community.

One afternoon, while reflecting on where she was at on her journey, she heard the words in her own voice say, "To get what you want, you must first be of service."

"I need to volunteer!" she thought.

She quickly went on craigslist to the community section to browse for an opportunity to volunteer.

Volunteers wanted for Gandhi's Birthday
and National Non-Violence Day

She gasped, "That's it!"

She responded to the listing, and coordinated her participation with the organizer.

She showed up the day of the event to be met with a frantic young man hurrying to get folding chairs out and in place. He was the nephew of the event's organizer and the other volunteer for the set-up of the event. They were both of Indian descent, and Emilee thought it fascinating that a cultural event like this was an opportunity for her to give back. She felt in her heart that this was where she was meant to be.

After setting up dozens of folding chairs and several tents, adding a feminine touch with some decorations, and arranging the flyers and t-shirts, Emilee took her place at the t-shirt table where she would interact with people as they joined the ceremony.

The two tents that set up next to her caught her eye. As if by magic, they were, The Vegetarian Society of Hawai'i and Down To Earth Organic and Natural grocery store. Satisfaction and joy entered her body as she felt the synchronistic connection of being in the right place at the right time. This truly was her opportunity to give herself to a cause and be rewarded from the Universe with exactly what she had been asking for.

When she had the time to meander around, she went up to those tables, looking at brochures and initiating conversation with the individuals. These were people with the same interests as her and they thought like she did about the food they ate.

"Where can I connect with more vegans?" she asked, explaining her desire to be part of a community.

The concept of "woofing" was explained, and how various sustainability farms on the islands allow work trade for the cost of living.

"Wow!" she thought, "I would love to live on a farm growing my own food and eating vegan."

At the end of the event, the man who had organized the gathering came up to Emilee and thanked her for her participation. "God chose you to be here today, girl, we really needed you," he said.

Delighted and bursting with purpose, she headed back home with a new dream in her head, "I am going to live on a sustainability farm."

That evening she went home to rest and reflect on the day's events. She went to sleep with gratitude in her heart for what had taken place. When she awoke the next morning, she checked craigslist for her next dream opportunity and listed there was:

Work traders to live and work on a sustainability farm

The farm was located on the Big Island, and although she had never been, she knew that was where she was going next. She applied, and after a Skype interview with one of the owners and the manager, was chosen to join the community. It was not completely free to live there; a small amount was owed for the accommodations on top of the hours worked, but a breakfast smoothie and lunch were included. Both meals were prepared by a vegan chef using as many sustainable resources from the farm as possible.

Only having enough money for her flight and one month's worth of accommodations, she took another leap of faith, trusting that it would fall into place for her.

It was evening when she arrived on the Big Island. "I hope they like me," she thought, as she waited for the person who would be bringing her to her temporary new home.

Arriving that evening to the sustainability farm deep in the jungle, there were not many city lights. In fact, the electricity was out on the part of the farm with her accommodations, so she was surrounded by darkness as she was dropped off at her bungalow tent. She was amazed by the illumination of the stars in the velvet black sky, but somewhat afraid of the surrounding darkness and the foreign sounds of the coqui frogs in the trees.

She recorded herself on video describing her arrival and posted it on social media. It seemed more frightening than it was, but she received overwhelming support from friends and family back home.

The kind words and support she had received throughout her entire journey in Hawai'i made her feel like a better person. "They see me for who I am now," she affirmed to herself, and it helped her to forget her past reputation.

After the first couple weeks of working on the farm, learning horticulture, eating chef-prepared vegan food, and practicing Yoga, the reality of Emilee's financial ability to stay was calling for her attention. How would she continue to live here? The question ran through her mind.

Shortly before her resources ran out, one of owners of the farm pulled Emilee into her office and began asking about her cooking experience. During the Skype interview, Emilee had shared her passion for cooking and the potluck parties she had thrown. The woman explained that the current chef was leaving and the substitute chef suddenly was not able to make it. She asked if Emilee would like to fill the chef position. The chef was not required to pay any cost of living as they worked the most hours.

"You are powerful, you know that?" she stated as she acknowledged how the events were working in favor of Emilee's extended stay.

Enthusiastically, Emilee accepted the position, knowing that everything was working out even better than she had hoped. Money was no longer a worry.

She would spend the next few months as the vegan chef for the community, harvesting food from the grounds and preparing plant-based meals. On the weekends she would take trips to the Farmer's Market for extra ingredients they were not growing yet. Five or six other members of the farm would accompany her, all of them riding in the back of a black pickup truck through the jungle roads.

Being of Service Exercise

Our passions and our purpose are interconnected. We may find that what we feel passionate about leads us towards our purpose. When we make choices out of passion and purpose, the Universe responds by giving us more of what we are passionate about and opportunities to apply our purpose. It is important to give back when we can. We can volunteer our time, donate money or items, and give freely of ourselves in a way that can benefit other people and the earth.

Giving of ourselves is a form of gratitude and thanking the Universe for the abundance you have received. You may experience being just what someone needed while getting exactly what you needed in return. Giving of yourself and donating is especially helpful if you feel unworthy of receiving. If you experience guilt or shame surrounding receiving, this can be a good exercise for you.

If you are in a career where you are of service already, consider if you have the energy and resources to offer a free session.

Do not give more of yourself than you are energetically or physically able to. Be generous when you can, and withdraw from giving when you need to. Find a balance within yourself of both giving and receiving. Do not give with the expectation to receive something in return but with the intention that you are balancing the parts of yourself that are masculine (giving) and feminine (receiving.)

See if there is a way you can be of service today or this week.

I have _____to donate to those in need.

_____ needs a helping hand and I am available to help.

I can offer _____ hours this week to be of service to my loved ones.

I could donate $_____to my favorite charity.

I can offer _____ free sessions and not be giving too much of myself.

Chapter 6 – Pressure Cooker

"The journeys you take and the adventures you lead are written in-depth in the scars that you see." ~ Emilee J. Kern

ALTHOUGH SHE ENJOYED COOKING for the community, Emilee found it difficult to plan a concrete menu for the week. Her cooking was purely intuitive; she would not know what she was preparing for lunch until she walked into the kitchen and visualized her idea. The creation flowed instinctively through her, and a delicious meal would result. She enjoyed her creative method, yet each night she stressed over her next creation, and each day magic would be made. Her method caused her slight anxiety, and after she wildly prepared the food in the kitchen, she rushed to get the food on the serving counter. Sometimes she enjoyed plating the food just so; she liked when everyone could experience her exact vision.

It was a normal day in the jungle kitchen, which was a giant screened-in greenhouse style structure on a cement platform. Chickens roamed wildly outside and fresh bananas from the grounds hung from rope on one side of the room. Baskets full of freshly picked citrus greeted the entryway, and jars of fresh coconut water lined the countertop.

For a plant-based food enthusiast, this was a heavenly place to be. The lunch menu of the day would be purple sweet potato soup in a vegetable broth served with quinoa and a green salad with lilikoi dressing.

That morning, the owner of the farm suggested Emilee begin using the pressure cooker for meals as it would speed up the process. Never having used one, she put all of her soup ingredients in the pot, sealed the lid, and went about her other duties while the meal cooked.

At a few minutes before noon, it was time to get the food on the serving bar and blow into the conch seashell to sound to the members of the community that lunch was served. Emilee had never gotten the blow of the conch correct and the terrible noise she executed only succeeded in making the farm dog howl.

Working in a panic to have everything ready, Emilee turned the dial to release the steam of the pressure cooker. Not considering the mechanics entirely, she tried to open the lid. She found the lid difficult to remove, and feeling pressed for time, began to force the lid open. She pushed the handles away from each other with all her might until the pan exploded with an unimaginable force. A horrifying popping noise could be heard as the lid hit the ceiling, thankfully going upwards and not towards her face or body. The boiling soup that had been cooking for over an hour followed the lid and blanketed Emilee's face and chest. A high-pitched shriek rang through the farm, far more successful at getting the community's attention than her conch shell blow had ever been.

Shocked and unable to move, Emilee bawled from the unbearable pain caused by the boiling water burning her flesh. An owner of the farm rushed in to investigate what had happened. He quickly grabbed a towel to wipe off the scalding liquid, and made a swift decision to remove the tank top that burned into her flesh. The farm manager followed in soon after, and having some first aid experience, they moved quickly to try to ease her pain. Still unable to move from shock and discomfort, she wept while the men tried to figure out what to do. First, they tried applying egg whites to the burns, and then raw tomato slices. They also tried oatmeal, and lastly, aloe vera.

Panic encircled her as they guided her to sit in a chair while applying the various food items on her burns. She could hear that someone had served up the soup amidst the commotion, and the community continued to eat as if it were a normal lunch break. Everyone could hear her cries, for all that separated them was a layer of tent and screen.

The owners discussed taking her to the hospital. They considered their options and offered her Ibuprofen. A loud sob broke the discussion after Emilee had been able to see one of the giant blisters forming where the strap of her tank top had held the hot soup the longest. It was gross and misshapen, bubbles on top of bubbles filled with fluid. Questioning if her face also looked like this, fear took over and she cried even more.

"Take me to the fucking hospital!" she finally asserted, standing up and facing the confused men.

Topless and shaking from shock and pain, Emilee hopped in the front seat of the little black pickup truck for the 30-minute drive to the hospital where she was treated and given medication for the wounds and pain.

The wounds healed quickly, and she was able to avoid staph infection while healing in the jungle. Covered in cream and bandages, she was able to take a few days off to rest and heal from the injury. Thankfully, her face healed without scarring, her chest carrying most of the visible proof. A few big keloids developed where the tank top had been, but Emilee wore her scars like a badge of honor. She was proud of herself for what she had accomplished so far. She felt nothing but gratitude and chose to keep moving forward.

She stayed on as the chef for a few more weeks following the accident. After her final duty of cooking for a retreat of guests visiting from Australia, she decided her time with the farm was complete. The private retreat guests stayed in the lodging accommodations on the farm and required a set daily menu during their visit. She made a small income from this opportunity and could afford a flight back to O'ahu to stay with the girl she had met on her first day at Duke's.

Surrendering Exercise

The farm that I lived on is located on the volcano of the Big Island of Hawai'i. I felt that the pressure cooker explosion was symbolic in its resemblance to a volcanic eruption.

Although I had achieved my desire of being part of a vegan community, and even a step above what I asked for by becoming the chef for the community, I was not at peace. It was stressful for me to plan a weekly menu; I felt a blockage when I tried. The only way I could create meals was to show up in the kitchen and let an idea flow through me intuitively.

It worked out 100 percent of the time, and the meals were always cooked well and delicious, but I was in a constant state of stress. I would experience anxiety at night or in the early morning before the idea came to me. As if I did not trust that it would work out as it did each day, I would worry, and the stress would accumulate. Once my shift was done, I would feel exhausted and relieved; I spent a lot of my free time crying in my bed.

I had two choices: I could menu plan and be prepared as I entered the kitchen each day, or trust in my abilities and approach each day with grace and ease. I chose to stay in the middle where I was, working under stress and forcing that pressure cooker to open. It exploded on my body as one boiling reminder to slow down, be present, and practice grace.

An affirmation that the group of Australian guests taught me was, "We are in the Jell-O."

For their retreat I was able to create a 3-meal daily menu, and it worked out really well. They requested a number of the meals to go, and some of the meals would be eaten fresh and at a scheduled time.

One evening I expected them for dinner at 7PM, as written on the retreat coordinator's daily agenda. The dinner was prepared, and the dishes all plated beautifully. I proudly admired my work, anxiously anticipating my happy guests' faces while they enjoyed the food. I grew impatient when they didn't arrive on time. I received a phone call that they were still 40 minutes away from the farm.

Annoyed, I scraped all the plates back into the serving dishes and accepted that all I could do was wait for their arrival.

When they finally arrived, they casually said, "We are in the Jell-O!"

"What the hell does that mean?" I thought.

They saw their day as formless, an open opportunity to explore and let things unfold as they would. They did not try to force anything, nor did they stress about the time. They would move with the circumstances and go with the flow.

I admired the idea, although I was slightly irritated because of the work I had put into having a meal prepared perfectly and on time. It was an important lesson for me, and a great close to my experience working as a chef and living on that sustainability farm.

Over the last few years, I have observed that my ability to be in the "Jell-O" while trusting the Universe is more likely with things such as finding the right job, moving into the right home, and circumstances working out in my favor. I struggle with being in the "Jell-O" during the smaller and more controllable moments of the day.

Consider if and when you are most likely to be in the "Jell-O" and going with the flow?

_____

_____

_____

_____.

When are you most likely to want structure and control?

_____

_____

_____

_____.

Is this something you would like to improve? _____

Who benefits when you are able to relax and go with the flow? Why?

_____

_____

_____

_____.

Are there times in your life when you could benefit from surrendering?

_____

If so, when?

_____

_____

_____

_____.

Chapter 7 – Synchronicities

"Whenever you acknowledge a synchronicity, you are strengthening your connection with the divine." ~ Unknown

FROM THE MOMENT I watched a film on the Law of Attraction, I have experienced numerous synchronicities. Many times, we chalk it up to coincidence and think, "Isn't that funny?" and proceed to brush off the occurrence. It is not too often that we stop to think about the possibility that we, in fact, attracted this scenario, and it is happening as a direct reflection of our thoughts and feelings.

The Law of Attraction teaches us that we create our reality with our thoughts. It seems unrealistic at first, and someone new to this idea might consider you silly for practicing it. Deep down I think we all wish to believe in magic and would believe if it presented itself to us. In order to experience it we must pay attention to the signs and listen to the messengers. When something seems coincidental or ironic, take a deeper look at what it is trying to tell you. The Universe is responding to you and answering your wishes all of the time.

Back in Wisconsin, the Law of Attraction subject began to come up everywhere. It was as if everyone I talked to had watched *The Secret* long before I did.

While practicing the exercises, I decided that I wanted to meet a man, and I had a very specific description of him. Within a few days of this exercise I went grocery shopping, and a man who fit the description approached me and literally followed me around the store the entire time I was shopping, talking about thinking positively and the Law of Attraction.

It was too outrageous for me to grasp at the time and I did not pursue this person. It was shocking how exact he fit my description, and that he began speaking about the LOA without prompt was unbelievable.

It was powerful; *I* was powerful. Life as I had known it had changed because I obtained a new awareness and a new understanding of how to create my reality.

In this chapter we are going to look at how to pay attention to messengers and listen to your own intuition. Perhaps after doing the exercises in the previous chapters, you have already begun to experience gut feelings or synchronistic encounters. Messages can come in forms such as songs on the radio, an online advertisement, random thoughts, calls from a person you just thought of, repeating numbers, or even a passing stranger might tell you exactly what you needed to hear. There are countless ways a message may be delivered to you. Do not disregard these messages or write them off as coincidence. Believe that a higher power is working with you.

Some people even practice asking for a specific sign and it works for them. They may say something like, "show me a single red rose today if _____ is in my best interest." Later that day they may see the most obvious red rose.

After watching a documentary on near-death experiences and how our deceased loved ones are still with us, I decided to give asking for a specific sign a try. Because I do not have any deceased loved ones with whom I was particularly close, I asked for a sign that my deceased dog Henley was still with me. Henley's favorite toy was a red rubber Frisbee; he was inseparable from it. I wrote in my journal that if he was with me to show me a sign of the red Frisbee he loved.

My current dog Loki was at a pet sitter's home the day I wrote this request in my journal. That evening I received several photo updates of the happy Beagle playing with the other dogs. Not expecting it, I was stunned to see photos of Loki proudly carrying the same brand of red rubber Frisbee that Henley had loved so much. Loki had gone to the same house a few days prior and I received lots of photos, none of which contained that red Frisbee.

I wept tears of joy and sadness when I received such an obvious confirmation that my Yellow Lab was still with me in this life.

My first deck of oracle cards came to me in a care package from one of my best Wisconsin friends while I was living in Waikiki. I would use these cards and many others for daily guidance over the next nine years and going forward. She was the first person to show me how to draw cards, and I drew them for the first time at her house before I moved to Hawai'i. I drew a card that read "daughter" and one of the meanings was: "an unborn baby girl is sending you her love."

I was struck as I had recently learned the news of my sister being pregnant with a girl. I felt something completely magical from reading that card, and connected to the energy of my soon-to-be niece.

~ ~ ~

Back on O'ahu, Emilee was envisioning what to do next. With her skin still pink from the burns she sustained from the eruption, she was taking time to nurture herself while considering what could be next. She had just had the most incredible experience living on the Big Island and working as a vegan community chef. What could possibly follow that?

While watching the sunset alone one evening, a thought came into her mind, "I could be a live-in nanny and cook for the family! That's how I would continue my journey here on the islands."

A friend had recently returned from a trip to the island of Maui, and hearing her tales of the island seized Emilee's attention. That's where she would go next, she declared, and began to visualize herself moving to Maui while she watched the sunset and felt grateful for everything she had endured so far. She knew that more magic was to come, and that she would be provided for.

After the sunset, Emilee returned to her friends' apartment, where she was temporarily staying. It was a Friday night, and the girls decided to walk around the busy town. Street performers would be out as well as hundreds of tourists. Military men would be swarming around the girls at the bars on the side streets tucked behind the main shops. The nightlife in Waikiki was alive most nights but amplified on Fridays. Fireworks would explode from the Hilton hotel that evening.

While walking through the busy streets and laughing with her friends, a single street performer caught their attention; a tarot card reader. Always enjoying intuitive messages, Emilee opted to have her cards read.

While reading her cards, the woman asked, "Have you thought about becoming a nanny?"

Not able to hold in her smile, Emilee giggled, as she knew this wonderful synchronicity was confirmation that becoming a nanny was the next step for her. She and her friends retreated back home after the readings and retired for the evening.

The next morning, Emilee woke up and knew exactly what she needed to do; check craigslist. Based on her past success, she knew this was a great way to find her next magical opportunity. She checked the *all islands* filter and immediately came across the listing meant just for her:

**Magical live-in nanny/vegetarian chef on Maui **

She laughed with delight as she knew this was meant to be. Emilee was going to move to Maui and live as an in-home nanny and cook for the family. It was perfect! She applied for the job and booked a ticket back to Wisconsin, as she knew that she wouldn't travel back home for a while once she moved to Maui.

She received a reply immediately and arranged a Skype interview while she was in Wisconsin. The family was also from the Midwest, and found Emilee to be a perfect match for their needs. The job started in a few weeks, so she spent the time in Wisconsin reconnecting with her friends and family.

During her first week back in Wisconsin, jet leg caused Emilee to stay awake later than normal. She was wide awake in the late hours of the night when she received a text from her sister, who was going into labor.

Excitedly and as quickly as she could, she drove to the hospital. She was going to be there for her sister and welcome her baby niece, who the oracle card affirmed she had a special connection to.

During the labor, there was a moment of uncertainty, and the baby's heart rate began to drop. Not knowing why she did it, Emilee walked over to her sister, placed her hand over her own heart and the other on her sister's wrist. Within seconds from the touch, the water broke, and meconium was in the fluid. The umbilical cord was around the baby's neck and it was time to act fast. Emilee carried a satchel of healing crystals and slid the sack under her sister's pillow before grabbing her left knee to assist her with her pushing. After just a few moments the healthy baby girl was born, relief and joy filled the room.

When Emilee held her niece, she could feel in her soul the deep and ancient connection they shared. She was grateful she could be there in that moment and experience that most spectacular event. What happened when Emilee touched her sister and her heart at the same time while the water broke simultaneously was never given a second thought. It could be viewed as one magical coincidence or perhaps there is a bit more to it than that.

Journaling Techniques and an Introduction to Oracle Cards

Use your journal to ask the Universe for specific signs and to keep a record of synchronistic events that take place. Once you begin to recognize the signs and messages they will happen more frequently. Use your journal to write out questions you may have, and also write any responses that come through your thoughts. This is a way to strengthen your intuition. Keeping track of every synchronistic event will encourage more events to flow to you.

Oracle cards are a wonderful tool to guide you on your path. They work via the Law of Attraction and any messengers in other dimensions that wish to guide and communicate with you. Some people believe that we have spirit guides, some believe in ancestral guidance, and others believe in angels. You may also set the intention to connect to your higher self when drawing cards. Whatever resonates with you is perfect when tuning into and drawing the cards.

When shopping for a deck, choose the one that calls to you. Some metaphysical shops will have open decks for you to sample. Take advantage of practicing with the open cards. Make sure the deck feels good to you when you hold it, read through the title and description of the cards, and notice intuitive expressions while you admire the artwork.

Each deck should be accompanied by a guidebook with examples of various types of readings you may do. You may also use your journal to write down intuitive messages you receive while drawing each card.

It was my vision to create an oracle deck using key lessons and words from the writings in this book so that my readers could deepen their daily practice of self-observation and manifestation skills. I have created a 44-card deck and guidebook titled *Monarch Manifestor Oracle Cards* that partners with the teachings in this book.

Chapter 8 – Gratitude

"The Universe is not making you wait. You are simply in the space between realizing where you're meant to be and feeling you're ready to go there. This is when you phase out of denial, release the anchors, the attachments, the false beliefs. This is not a punishment for being unfinished, it's a sacred part of your journey. You are not stuck. You are just becoming the person who can finally take the leap."
~ Brianna Wiest

IT WAS DARK when her plane arrived on Maui. Dazed by the lights of the city of Kahului and exhausted from her travel, she was grateful and nervous to arrive at her new home. The father of her new live-in nanny position would be picking her up from the airport. Anxious thoughts arose with the idea of meeting the new stranger she would be living with, cooking for, and caring for his children.

"I hope they like me." she thought.

Upcountry Maui was one of the most beautiful places she had ever been. Located at 3,000 feet above sea level, the air is cool and the heat of the sun was most welcomed during the early mornings and late afternoons.

Emilee quickly adjusted to her daily duties of meal preparation, household chores, and driving the children to and from school. Although the family was vegetarian, she tried to prepare most of their meals vegan. She had purchased a juicer and began drinking fresh juices daily. It was peaceful on the mountain, and she found herself able to sit quietly between duties and soak in the scenery.

In the late mornings when the house was quiet and she was alone, she could sip her juice and reflect on the last several months of her journey. Her giant leap of faith had led her to this exact moment, as well as all the parts of herself she was not so proud of. None of it was separate from whom she was today. She had shared much of her journey on social media, and without a phone, she used an iPod connected to Wi-Fi to share videos and posts of her experience. The people she had left behind were cheering her on as she shared and followed her dreams. It felt good to be seen for who she was now while inspiring them to go after their own dreams.

During her mornings, she appreciated the stillness. Walking around barefoot she would admire the vivid colors of the flowers and succulents. Every time a butterfly would flutter by, her heart reached forward as if to dance alongside it. There was so much beauty to be seen and cherished, and she took it in daily. At night she would gaze through her skylight at the moon and the stars, particularly a bigger star that always seemed to follow her no matter where she went. It flickered green and purple and seemed to talk to her with each flare. It was when she was gazing at these natural phenomena that she could feel her inner guidance the most.

Emilee felt joyful living on Maui. She was glowing from her daily juices and time spent in solitude. She spent each day quietly thinking about the things that brought her joy. She wrote "Thank You Juice" on her mason jar, and said, "Thank you," each time she drank her juices, smoothies or water from it. She painted an old coffee can and wrapped the outside in a hand-drawn mural mirroring her view of the valley down below. Inside the can she planted a dino kale start, and wrote affirmations of gratitude around the mural.

As if that moment never happened to her at age 12 when she stopped believing in the magical possibilities of a higher power, she now knew the truth. Life was magical, and it was up to her to experience it. It was through faith, trust, and gratitude that she had gotten to this point in her life. The synchronistic events that happened at perfect times allowed her to become dependent on the Universe. She was never afraid and did not worry about lack; she was always provided for.

She did not venture out right away or explore the island of Maui in the first few months of living there. Having a car to use was a blessing, but Emilee experienced slight intimidation and insecurity from her new scars. Instead she spent most of her free time alone, painting and dreaming, giving gratitude for what the Universe had given her so far. This was a time for solitude and contemplation. The sizable keloids that developed after her burns healed felt like a third eye on her forehead. She was torn between feeling ashamed and feeling grateful for the experience.

One day she ventured out to the beach and stared glassy-eyed towards the ocean pondering, "When will I meet my soulmate?" as she did so often. "Will someone ever love me? Not with these scars," she thought.

Her heart was sad as she felt alone on her journey; although magical, it was often lonely for her. She was always longing to meet "the one."

A voice broke her silent conversation with herself. "Don't worry, someone will love you."

She looked up to see a woman looking down at her as if reading her thoughts. "They aren't that bad," the woman affirmed, nodding towards her scars.

Emilee forced a half smile, feeling sorry for herself yet grateful for the confirmation she had just received that her soulmate was in fact on the way.

"But when?" Emilee sighed impatiently.

Visualization Practice

Gratitude is the key to manifesting your desires, opportunities, and being able to hear important messages. With gratitude we trust, believe, and are open to receiving. Saying, "Thank you, Universe," is an affirmation in itself that what you wish for is coming.

Think about the number one thing in your life that you are grateful for. Take a moment to ponder this; it may be a person, an object, place, or experience. Scan your body and see if you notice where you feel the source of gratitude. Perhaps you feel your heart expanding or a warmness in your lower belly. There is no wrong place, just feel into the sensations of your body. Once you have it, take note of this feeling.

Now make a list of 10 things you are grateful for. When going through the list, notice in your body if you feel the same sense of gratitude. If the same feeling is not present, go through the list again, and consciously try to send the energy to your gratitude center. It may be helpful to say why you are grateful as well.

Try this:

I am grateful for _____

because _____.

Next, think of an area of your life you where would like improvement or modification. Instead of focusing on what you do not like about the situation, try visualizing how you would like it to be.

Remember that we are attracting our thoughts, and if we say, "I do not want my spouse to _____," we are focusing on what we do not want, and this will manifest more into our lives, as well as more disturbance from us surrounding the situation.

If we can shift our focus to, "I am grateful when my spouse _____;" insert opposite action, we are focusing on more of what we do want. This will help shift our feelings into a state of gratitude for our spouse and appreciation when they are doing what we are grateful for.

Another example could be when you believe there is never a parking spot when you go to your favorite shop. We are sending this image and message to the Universe that there are never any parking spots, which sends the vibration of lack and fear to the Universe. It is likely that you will always have trouble finding a parking spot.

If we shift this to an affirmation, "I always have the perfect parking spot when I go to _____. Thank you, Universe, for my perfect parking spot." Then imagine yourself driving in your car and the excitement you feel while pulling into your parking spot. You may even try for a specific parking spot if you wish.

During this practice, I have struggled with truly trusting that there will be a free parking spot. Anxiety would take over, and although I would visualize the parking spot, doubt would sit at the pit of my stomach.

I have shifted my experience from anxiety and doubt to a feeling of excitement. I tell myself, "I am excited to go to _____, and am so happy that I have a parking spot." This gives my brain an emotion to replace the anxiety. Whatever it is you are feeling grateful for, invite the same sensation to flow through your body.

Focus on feeling joy while saying your affirmations. Joy is a combination of happiness and being thankful. The emotion of joy is a powerful tool when aligning your vibration with what you want to manifest.

Think of an object that can be your reminder to be grateful.

For me, the moon triggers my gratitude response. Whenever I see the moon, no matter the phase or time of day, it grabs my attention and a deep sense of gratitude expands from my heart center. I take a few seconds to appreciate its beauty and to realign with my heart center. The moon evermore reminds me to be grateful.

Another symbol of gratitude for me is the Monarch butterfly. The Monarch takes me back to my third grade classroom where we were able to observe a full metamorphosis cycle from caterpillar through chrysalis and butterfly. I remember the smell of the netted cage housing tiny spotted caterpillars and the anticipation that built up as they hung inside their mint-green casing before releasing themselves to this world as transformed individuals.

Imagine if a butterfly had an ego, the entitlement they may carry with this ability to transform into one of the most appreciated insects on the planet. They are imperial and deserve a noiseless moment of appreciation.

I have noticed a pattern in my home gratitude practice when it comes to my wanting to change location. Over the last several years, and including when I left my home in Wisconsin, anytime I was trying to manifest a big move, it wasn't until after I surrendered and was truly comfortable in a house or in my circumstance that the new opportunity would manifest.

It wasn't until recently that I realized this comfort was a form of gratitude for what I did have. Sometimes it would come in the form of painting a room, rearranging furniture, or eliminating clutter. It may be that I created a special place in the home that was just for me. I may have found the job I wanted or made friends I longed for, but once I had that feeling of utter comfort and I relaxed in my current surroundings without yearning for more, the next opportunity to move would present itself.

Being grateful for what you currently have and not focusing on what you do not have is a key part to manifesting more. "Good things come when you least expect it" could be interpreted as "Good things come when you are not focusing on them not coming and appreciate what you have in each moment." This does not mean we can't wish for more. In the next chapters we will look at making our list and using visualization techniques to manifest them. Then we will send gratitude to what we already have and what we wish to have.

Chapter 9 – This or Something Better

"We honor the dream by doing the work." ~ Cleo Wade

"**YOU SHOULD CHECK OUT** the Kombucha bar," her house dad suggested. "They have raw vegan food, and it's a good hangout for people your age. You may have luck meeting friends there."

A friendly suggestion, as Emilee was interested in meeting some friends and getting out on the island. She imagined what this Kombucha bar may be like. Still slightly intimidated to immerse herself into the community, she fantasized about going there; surely that was where she would meet her soulmate.

She had successfully made one friend on Maui while working for that family. One morning after dropping the children off at school, she received word that there was another nanny her age with a child in the same class. Emilee spotted the other nanny during pickup, and discovered that she was also from Wisconsin.

"So, would you like to be friends?" Emilee shyly asked, but knew for sure they could bond over their Wisconsin lineage and present-day circumstances.

The girls hit it off, and they took to the beach on occasion and even ventured together to a ladies' night at a local pub. Things were beginning to become more comfortable on Maui.

The nanny gig was a short-term position while Emilee helped the family welcome a newborn baby boy. The family decided to spend their summer back on the mainland, so it was up to her to find a new place to live and work.

Continuing with her passion as a vegan chef, Emilee produced business cards to help her find a new opportunity. Buying a pack of 50, she only ever handed out one card - to one of the children's teachers, while explaining her need for a new nanny position.

Within days of needing to find a new opportunity, Emilee received a phone call from a family who were expecting a new baby. The teacher had overheard their conversation about possibly needing help and gave them Emilee's card. As friendly as could be, the dad made plans to pick her up and move her to their home where she would have a similar work-trade arrangement.

This time the agreement was a little different as to the amount she earned, and she had to work a bit more to earn the rent. She started to lose interest in cooking for other people and decided it was time to look for an additional job.

Her new house dad called a nearby restaurant owner and said, "I have a girl for you."

Emilee went in for an interview, and after hearing that she was from Wisconsin, the owner claimed to love hard-working Midwest folks; she was hired.

After weeks of working at the restaurant, Emilee wanted to commit herself full time to the serving job and transition to paying rent outright. She searched for a new place to rent that was more reasonable. She found the perfect room to rent in a two-bedroom cottage that was walking distance from the restaurant. Her new roommate was a woman in her early sixties, a beautiful woman with a rich social life on the island. Emilee found it peaceful to live with this woman; she enjoyed working her shifts and coming home to rest, occasionally having enlightened conversations with her roommate.

The Kombucha bar was across the street from the restaurant and Emilee enjoyed going there after her shifts. Her confidence had improved after meeting coworkers at the restaurant and sharing after-shift beverages, much like the previous Wisconsin years.

She was grateful for the way opportunities presented themselves to her through a tight community-based web of people on the island.

With one eye always on the lookout for that perfect guy, Emilee made a list of what she wanted to manifest in a partner. She wrote out several categories in her journal: looks, personality, spirituality, money, values, family, career, and miscellaneous. She wrote down in detail how her man would look, his interest in travel and the freedom to do so. She wanted a man who was close with his family and wanted children of his own. He would be open to her spirituality beliefs. He would be easy-going and up for adventure. He should also have blond hair and blue eyes like her. She had a soft spot for these men. His body would not be too hairy, as she didn't like it.

For many weeks she dreamt of meeting "the one." An occasional dating app failure would come, and she found these men to be socially awkward. The dating pool was tough, and the men were not like those she knew back home. She could walk into any bar in her hometown and easily be offered a free drink and a smile. Here, everyone seemed to keep to themselves, only holding conversation with those they knew.

Trying one more time at dating, she met a young man while working a shift at the restaurant. He was completely casual with her, but out of desperation she wanted to see it for more than what it was. This was the first time she had attempted to date someone who did not fall in love with her immediately. Ignoring the signs, she casually went on dates until it was brought to her attention who else he was dating.

She ended the encounters and completely gave up on finding her man. Feeling hopeless and ready for a change, she decided it was time to kick the Universe into action and quit her job. She knew if she made a decision, a new opportunity would fall into place.

"I'm finished with my lessons here; I am ready to quit." Emilee told her coworkers.

"It's not about lessons; it's about making money," a coworker responded.

Emilee knew that it didn't matter, an opportunity would arise and the money would come. There were several times when she was down to her last few dollars; she had even given those dollars away to another person in need. She would always have enough, she affirmed.

Her boss laughed with understanding when she explained why she was quitting. "Well, if a new opportunity doesn't arise, you can stay working here."

Emilee appreciated the support.

A new opportunity quickly came her way. An old friend from Wisconsin had moved to the island and asked her to be his roommate. The new location was clear across the island and it was perfect. Emilee accepted the offer and gave her current roommate a notice. This was the change she was looking for.

Creating a Wish List

Use a similar list when manifesting your perfect partner, job, home, opportunity, or any other experience.

Include every possible detail you can think of. Consider textures, smells, sounds, and most importantly, how you will feel when you manifest the person or object. Take time to visualize this daily and be sure to experience it through your own eyes, utilizing your senses throughout the exercise.

Begin by deciding where you would like to create this list. Write it in a journal, on the computer, or take notes on your phone. You may write them out by category one at a time.

You do not have to use the example questions if they do not resonate with your desires. If you are uncertain of what you want, you may write what you think it might be and add: "this or something better."

Continue to add to the list as you think of more details.

Take your time and consider the exercise we did in Chapter 3. Make sure to focus on what you do want and not on what you do not want. Write down exactly what this looks like. Imagine it from your perspective, as if you are seeing it through your own eyes. See the shifter of your new car and feel the leather of the seat under your buttocks. Smell the scent of a new vehicle and the excitement you feel when driving off the car lot. Feel the joy as you turn the key in the lock of your new home and the texture of the floor under your feet. Feel the love and contentment you will feel when you find your perfect partner.

Gather as many details about every subject as you can imagine.

Be thorough in listing your desires. If it's a perfect mate, list how they look, their family life, spirituality, values, money, goals, etc. If you want a partner who is adventurous and health-conscious, wants to have children later in life, and will love your pet dog like their own, write it all down! Think of every possible detail. We will be using this list to visualize and manifest, so leave no detail behind.

I'm serious! I wanted a spouse without body hair, and I only visualized a bare chest. My husband has a bare upper body but the hairiest legs ever.

Affirming "this or something better" allows room for your manifestations to arrive better than you could imagine. If your manifestation arrives and it hasn't ticked every box on your list, avoid feeling discouraged. If it feels right, then it is right for you. It is likely that what has manifested is in your best interest, and the scenario may require your involvement, growth, and lessons before it becomes exactly as you want it.

For example: I did want my husband to be vegan, it was on my list. He was not vegan when I met him and eventually, I gave up the lifestyle choice. Seven years later, he decided he wanted to give veganism a try and together we changed our lifestyle. I also wanted him to have blond hair and blue eyes, but over the years I realized that I quickly get bored with the looks of blond-haired, blue-eyed men. I am very intrigued and attracted to my husband's dark hair and eyes. I believe someone knew better than I when aligning me with my soulmate.

I am not suggesting you settle for less than you want or deserve, but be open to something greater than you can imagine for yourself.

Perfect Partner; Home; Career; Finances; Vehicle

Example List Questions:
My Perfect Partner:
- **Looks:** What do they look like physically?
- **Beliefs:** Are they religious or hold any specific spiritual beliefs?
- **Values:** What is important to them?
- **Family:** Are they close with their family? Do they have or want children?
- **Relationships:** How are they with their friendships, coworkers, ex-relationships?

- **Health:** What standard of health to they have and how do they maintain it? Are they health-conscious?
- **Finances:** How much money do they earn and how are they with spending?
- **Extra-curricular:** What do they do for fun? Are they adventurous?
- **Personality:** Are they outgoing, funny, easy-going, etc.?
- **Affection:** How affectionate are they?

Dream Home:
- **Location:** Where is the home located? *Consider the neighborhood and surrounding visuals like water or trees.*
- **Size and design:** How many square feet is the home? How many bedrooms and bathrooms does it have? How big is the garage? What colors are the outside of the home? *Consider every detail about the home's appearance.*
- **Interior:** What textures and colors are on the inside of the home? What accents and details does it have?
- **Comfort:** How do you feel inside your new home?
- **Decor:** How will you decorate your new home? *Reword for remodeling your current home.*

Career:
You can change your questions to relate to a stay-at-home parent or business owner.
- **Income:** How much income would you like to earn?
- **Clients:** What does your perfect client look like?
- **Schedule:** What is your ideal schedule? Do you want more flexibility?
- **Time off:** Determine your desired amount of vacation time.
- **Co-workers:** Consider what your ideal relationship with your co-workers or partners looks like.
- **Passion:** Does your job bring you passion and purpose?
- **Energetic:** Do you feel energized by your job? Is there a balance of how much you are giving and receiving?

Finances:
- **Amount:** How much money do you want to see in your bank account?

- **Residual**: How much money would you like to earn in your account, and how often would you like it deposited?
- **Spending**: How will you spend your money?
- **Earning**: How will you earn this money? *The Universe isn't just going to fill your bank account, but will show you ways to increase your income.*
- **Giving back**: How can you contribute to others with your money?

Vehicle:
- **Make/Model**: What is your dream car or the car you want now?
- **Color**: What color is your new car?
- **Interior**: What material and color is the interior of your new vehicle?
- **Extras**: Are there any special features on this particular model? Are you buying the upgraded package?
- **Usage**: Where will you drive your new vehicle?

Next, attach a positive emotion to each experience.
"I am joyously driving in my new car."
"I am passionately working at my new job as a _____."
"I achieved a pay increase with grace and ease."
"I am filled with joy as I receive $_____ in my bank account each month."
"I am filled with excitement as I have enough money to spend on _____."
"The love between my partner and I is abundant."
"Joy and ease surround my experience."
"I feel relaxed and comfortable in my home."

These are all examples, and I encourage you to write similar sentences to go along with the subjects you are focusing on. You are free to choose the areas of your life you wish to emphasize. If you would like to choose one or two things to focus on first, go ahead and honor that. When going forward with your Vision Board, you can also focus on these areas and come back to the others later. Any time you want to revisit an area in your life, come back to the practice of making a list.

Chapter 10 – Perceptions

"You are a spiritual being. You are energy, and energy cannot be created or destroyed – it just changes form. Therefore, the pure essence of you has always been and will always be." ~ The Secret

WHILE SITTING IN THE GARDEN of the upcountry home where she was the nanny, Emilee spent her downtime visualizing and feeling grateful for her future. She had a deep sense of knowing that her every wish would come to fruition. She had watched it happen over and over again. She had no reason to doubt the Universe and its desire to co-create with her.

It was here that Emilee had the inspiration to create her first Vision Board. She collected markers, paints, and construction paper and fashioned two light blue sheets of construction paper together to make a medium-sized poster board. With markers she drew images and wrote words of things she wanted to manifest. At the top and center of her board was the most important item: her "Soulmate." Underneath "Soulmate" read "Travel to Europe;" somewhere off to the side it said, "Travel to Thailand." "Write a book" was also prevalent with a small doodle of a book.

She took time considering each word she wrote and visualizing the manifestation of them. Often, she would gaze at her Vision Board and go over her list of her perfect man. He was coming, she was sure; it was just a matter of when.

Almost a year after creating her Vision Board she sat at the Kombucha bar, finishing one of her last post-shift jars of "booch," her future man no longer on her mind. She had truly given up for now, and was moving across the island. It was time to focus on a different beginning.

It was this certainty that didn't even make her think twice when "he" sat down next to her that evening.

Seated to her right, a dark-haired, brown-eyed young man joined the local patrons. She hadn't seen him in here before. The friend she was with had left, and she was just finishing up herself. She chose to tune into the conversation between the smiley booch-tender and the young man, and she made out that he was from Europe. His dark hair was soft with subtle curls, a dimple on his left cheek made him look kind, and the way his black shirt clung to his biceps made him a nice-looking young man.

"A good-looking younger guy from Europe…" she thought with smile. "He must have the girls going wild for him." She chuckled to herself, thinking there wasn't any reason to think more about this person. She left that evening and headed back to her shared cottage for a night's rest.

After her shift the following day, Emilee again found herself seated at the bar drinking her ritualistic post-shift jar of booch. She wasn't surprised when the empty seat next to her was taken, and quickly noted that it was a young man wearing a white surfer t-shirt, headphones strung around his neck, and a black baseball hat covering his dark curly hair. A sense of familiarity and peace came over her as she recognized the European guy from the previous night.

The kombucha at this bar was highly "elevating" as they called it. The natural fermentation mimicked an alcoholic response called a "booch buzz." This gave the place a high vibrational atmosphere with chatty people vibing on the kombucha and raw vegan foods.

The energy of the booch and the atmosphere pulsed through her as she turned to talk to this nice-looking younger man. She introduced herself, the thought of him possibly being interested never crossing her mind; in fact, she wasn't interested. She categorized him as the typical Maui guy who had his choice of beautiful bronzed young women flocking to the booch bar. She didn't see herself as one of them. Her gnarly keloid scars and her past were still lingering deep inside saying, "You're not worthy."

Now that he was sitting close, she began to survey him a little more. She recognized his dimple that made him look friendly, and now she could smell his cologne. The most surprising thing about him were his hands, soft and gentle. Her father was a master carpenter and his fingers were that of one. His nails were thick, and fingers worn with years of working with his hands. Being of Viking descent and having a few rough years behind her, she took these gentle hands as another sign that this person was not for her.

She was surprised how easily the conversation unfolded between the two of them. Because she wasn't considering him to be her potential soulmate, she spoke freely, without hesitation. She did not try to impress him and didn't care what he would think of her. It was nice to have this conversation, and quite exciting to her that he was from Switzerland.

At eight o'clock, the bar closed down and the two took their conversation outside. Minutes flew by effortlessly as their dialogue continued. They discovered that they frequented the same beach, and made arrangements to meet there at 2PM the next day.

Arriving promptly at the beach, she laid out her towel. Soaking up the sun, she was excited for her meet-up. It was nice to have had that easy conversation the previous night. This guy was so kind and showed little evidence of an ego. But he was five years younger than her, and he surely was looking for a younger girl in a size extra-small bikini. She was medium-sized, and her body was built strong.

Her inner dialogue was interrupted by a nearby conversation in an unfamiliar language. The Swiss guy was standing over the nearest couple, also from his country, and they were chatting in their native tongue.

Certain that he had seen her, she relaxed in the sun, waiting for him to finish his conversation. She sat up feeling disappointed as she watched him walk away in the other direction after the discussion. "Typical flakey dudes!" she thought.

People could be casual here; they often made plans and followed up with an "eh, if it happens it happens."

She quickly gathered her things, stung by the reality that he wasn't serious about their plans, and decided to leave the beach slightly embarrassed, as if anyone had known she was just blown off.

"Yell his name," she thought, and yelled, "Beni!!!!" across the beach.

He turned around and smiled, and walked towards her. "I forgot my glasses," he clarified, relieved that he had found her.

He truly had not seen her a few feet away from the couple he was exchanging conversation with minutes prior.

Both relieved and excited to enjoy their afternoon together, they sat in the warm sand. They continued to share more about themselves, swapping interests and experiences.

"Why are you digging in the sand like that?" he asked.

She hadn't realized it, but she was nervously digging holes with her feet and hands as she talked. "I don't know," she chortled, cheeks flushed.

They found out about each other's dating status, and he stated he would like to meet a girl while he was visiting. The way he said it made Emilee believe that he was on the lookout, but elsewhere.

She saw him as a friend who could use her help finding girls. "You should join my friends and I tomorrow at open mike night; I'll be your wingman."

He agreed to join her for the evening. Confident in her ability to talk to people, she saw herself introducing him to single young ladies who would be at the bar.

The next evening, he picked Emilee from the restaurant she worked at.

"You look beautiful!" he said when he met the gaze of her blue eyes.

She had taken some time to blow-dry her naturally wavy hair and put it into curls. She even wore a fiery-red lipstick. She was ready for an evening of fun with her friends, and to play the role of a matchmaker for this young Swiss guy.

What Emilee thought would be a casual night of socializing turned into a triple date. Two other couples joined them, and they all shared a table at the bar. Emilee enjoyed her usual Jameson, while her date drank a lemonade.

"I don't drink and drive," he explained to the group, who each consumed an alcoholic beverage.

As the evening went on, that Swiss boy and Wisconsin girl exchanged glances and laughs.

"Why is he winking at me?" she thought, "Is he winking at everyone?"

Between laughs and stories, they would lock eyes and he would wink at her. It took her by surprise.

"He isn't looking around for another girl, he is fully engaged, sober, and he keeps winking at me."

Taking it lightly, she didn't want to overthink it, and continued to enjoy the evening.

After calling it a night, the two drove back to Emilee's home. She instructed him to be quiet by turning off the engine and lights so as to not wake her sleeping roommate. She thanked him for the wonderful evening and said goodbye, offering him an Aloha hug.

Hugging in Hawai'i is a common way to say hello and goodbye, and it was her way of telling him that she had fun. Before she could put her arms all the way around, she was startled when his lips met hers. She was truly surprised; she did not see it coming. Either she had been completely oblivious to all of his signals or intentionally tried to play it cool the entire time, but it was happening now. He was interested in *her*. They spent a little more time exchanging passionate kisses before saying goodbye for the evening.

Identifying Judgements

By allowing my own perceptions of other people and judgements towards myself to influence my thoughts, I was unable to see the clarity of the events that were unfolding in front of me. If I had listened to these beliefs and not gone after him that day at the beach, it is possible that our connection would not have happened.

I later found out that he returned that next day to the Kombucha bar at the exact same time hoping to see me. The first night he sat next to me, he was previously at a table and took the first open bar seat when it became available, hoping to sit closer to me. I was too concerned with my wounded ego to see the beauty of what was truly manifesting.

I am happy with the way these events unfolded because I was very authentic and did not withhold anything of myself with him.

Our perceptions and judgements influence our experience. If we can shift our perspective towards a person or situation by removing our own beliefs and baggage from it, we may allow it to unfold organically for what it is, not what we think it should be. This act of applying our own "stuff" to a situation comes from our ego. Our ego is what keeps us safe; it is trying to protect us from our past hurts reoccurring.

Reflect on some of your own beliefs towards a person or experience. In what ways have your judgements influenced this belief? Your perceptions may feel like solid truth, but are likely a combination of your past experiences and judgements preventing you from witnessing the simple truth of the situation.

Let's reflect on a bit of my experience, reviewing what was true and what was actually my own perception of the truth.

True Statement: Beni was a young man from Switzerland.
My perception/judgement: Beni was a young man from Switzerland, therefore he already had a lot of nice-looking girls interested in him.

True Statement: Beni has two hands.

My perception/judgement: Beni's hands looked soft and gentle. His hands represent his inability to handle a woman who has as many scars as myself.

True Statement: There are young women on Maui.
My perception/judgement: The young women on Maui are beautiful. I am not as beautiful, therefore do not stand a chance to find a man.

These are examples from my specific story. If there is a person or situation that causes you unrest, ask yourself what the truth of the situation is, and separate your beliefs about that person and situation from the truth.

Another exercise I suggest is to Google your most frequented restaurant. Take a look at the reviews from other people's experiences. It could be that not everyone cherishes this restaurant the same way you do. If there are negative reviews, imagine if someone was trying to convince you not to go to this restaurant because the service was terrible and the food was bad. This opinion is based completely from their own personal experience. It does not mean that their opinion isn't valid, it only means they did not enjoy their experience. Perhaps the chef had a bad day, or the waitress felt off; many things could go wrong in a restaurant. The person who wrote the review could have been having a bad day in general and projected their emotions onto the dining experience. Perhaps you have been to this restaurant dozens of times and have never had a bad experience, or perhaps maybe have experienced a situation that you forgave because you had empathy towards the situation and because you know that the typical experience at this establishment is not this way.

Our choices and preferences are based off our own opinions and experiences. I'm not suggesting you never read through reviews when choosing a new restaurant. My example was metaphoric for how what is true for one person may not be true for another. Observe when you may be projecting your own beliefs on to others and how that may alter their experience.

Chapter 11 – "Ke Nalu Nei Ka Moana"

"The Ocean is Full of Waves." ~ Hawaiian Proverb

I WAS 21 WHEN I experienced my first pregnancy. I worked full time as a Dental Assistant, and was in a relationship much like the others I mentioned. I was not completely happy with the man I was dating, yet I went through the motions of having a home together, working a "real job," and doing what I thought I was supposed to.

After having had irregular menstrual symptoms, I went to my OB, only to discover I was pregnant.

"Ms. Nicholson, you're pregnant…" was the answer I heard on the phone with the test results.

While shocked at the possibility, as I was on birth control, excitement quickly took over. The irregular bleeding warranted an ultrasound, and the bloodwork determined that it was an ectopic pregnancy. This condition was foreign to me, I had never heard of such a pregnancy. The news came just days before Thanksgiving, so I was scheduled to receive my injection of methotrexate to eliminate the embryo the day following the holiday. At the time I did not call it an embryo, it was "my baby." Joined by my sisters and mother, that Friday was exceptionally black. Several days after my injection, I began to experience crippling abdominal cramps.

"Take another Vicodin," a nurse instructed from the phone.

I was sitting on the toilet, experiencing an intense amount of pain that a painkiller would not touch. Relief came when my doctor called and urged that I immediately come to the emergency room. Another assistant drove me to the hospital, and I was greeted with emergency surgery. My fallopian tube had burst, and I was bleeding internally. An examination of the removed tube concluded that my fallopian tube was underdeveloped and unable to pass the cells through.

"There is a good chance the other tube is the same; we will not know until we do additional testing," the doctor explained.

I would go on to spend most of my days desperately wanting to conceive a child.

~ ~ ~

"Hi, Emilee, it's Swiss Ben. May I come see you today?"

A common text from her new beau.

She was surprised how easily their relationship developed. She never had to question his intentions and there weren't any games to see through. He was genuinely interested in devoting the rest of his vacation to her. She was in-between jobs and had just moved to the other side of the island with her friend so she could dedicate her time as well to growing this new relationship. He would drive 45 minutes each way from the North Shore all the way to the Westside. She could not believe he did that just to see her; if you move to the other side of the island, years can go by without seeing people you knew from the opposite side.

Weeks went by and the duo enjoyed the romance that blossomed between them. It was so easy, and they got along so well. Emilee was surprised that she was never shy around him. She had been herself the entire time.

"I'm on my way," a text read as she was preparing for a date with him one afternoon.

She sat crossed-legged on the floor as she smoothed on a shimmering lip gloss while gazing into the closet door mirror. She appreciated how tan her skin was; it was extra glowing today.

"This must be what it looks like to be in love," she thought. "Hmmm," she observed, as she realized her bust had gotten bigger. She had been indulging in chocolate desserts and wine at many of their dinner dates. Perhaps she was gaining weight. "My eyes are so blue!" she noted, as she met her own stare. Her stomach grew in knots as she put everything together and came to a conclusion. "I'm pregnant!" she said, as this wisdom that began in her gut made itself clear in her mind.

Fear came over her. How would she tell him what she had concluded? Innocently, she had thought she would never get pregnant because of her fallopian tube abnormality.

Later that evening she found the courage to ask him to take her to a drugstore. "I think I may be pregnant...."

The color left his face with the statement, and she knew this was not something he was ready to hear. He wasn't staying here forever, he had to return to his home in another few weeks. Their conversation continued in the parking lot of the store, and she was humiliated by the smirks of two women who overheard his reaction to the situation.

They quickly drove back to the house to take the test. She activated the stick and entered the shower to have a minute to herself. After a few minutes she opened the shower door and reached for the stick before grabbing a towel. Two obvious pink lines stared back at her, and in that moment her heart dropped. This was what she wanted more than anything in the world, but not quite like this, and not so soon into this relationship.

Although unplanned and uncertain how they would move forward with the news, the feelings between them were the same. They had already discussed a possible future and teased about having to get married to be together.

She was amazed by the way she felt towards him. She could never remember an exact moment that she felt she was falling in love. The love between them was instant and as if it always was. It was not separated by time; it felt the same from the moment they first met to any other time in their relationship. She felt unconditional love, understanding and an unexplainable connection to him. He was not blond-haired or blue-eyed like she had asked the Universe on her list, but he was uniquely him and it was right; she knew it.

Within a day of receiving the news of pregnancy, Emilee began to experience light cramping and spotting. Fear came over her as she recalled her previous ectopic pregnancy. She would not go through that again. There was absolutely no way the Universe would put her through that again. She had gone through that lesson already. She wanted more than anything that this pregnancy was meant to be.

The couple headed to the ER to be certain. After four hours in the waiting room with them both sitting in silence and anticipation, they were called to be seen. An ultrasound and blood test were done to determine the state of the pregnancy. Sporting a hospital gown and laying reclined in the bed, Emilee held back the tears as she prayed to be pregnant.

"Ms. Nicholson, you are pregnant. We cannot see the embryo on the ultrasound, and there is a 50-50 chance that it is ectopic."

That 50 percent of hope was all she needed to hear. Without consulting Beni or considering his thoughts, she spoke, "I want to keep my baby. I want to keep it."

Understanding the desperation, the doctor allowed her to return home without any action with the agreement that she would get labs drawn every few days to make sure the pregnancy was progressing and not ectopic.

Over the next few days the labs were not consistently increasing. The numbers were not doubling as they should, but Emilee did not give up hope. He had only a few days left on the island before his visa expired, and they spent their days in uncertainty.

Finally, one of the lab results provided a glimpse of hope. The numbers had grown, and it was possible that the pregnancy was viable. Overjoyed that there was a chance, Emilee was optimistic about her future with the baby and Beni. Uncertain how everything would work itself out, she trusted that it would.

She was scheduled for a follow up ultrasound after he left the island. She laid reclined with the cool leather chair underneath her, and nervously glanced around the room. A printed sign with the words "Molon Labe," caught her eye.

During his time on the island, Beni had gotten this tattooed on his arm, representative of his own journey and the hardship he had overcome. He had arrived in Maui in a wheelchair, unable to walk for the six months prior to his trip. After specialists all over his country had come up empty-handed, he had come to Maui to see a body worker who got him walking out of the wheelchair in a matter of days. They met shortly after; this was the reason for his visit.

Molon Labe. Come and Take. It was a confirmation that no matter what, she would be ok. A sign from the Universe that synchronistic happenings were still unfolding, and Beni was with her.

It was a different doctor than the one who performed the first ultrasound in the ER. "I am sorry, but this is certainly an ectopic pregnancy. It was clearly an ectopic pregnancy from day one, and we should have taken care of this at the emergency room."

Her heart nose-dived as if it could have dropped straight to the ground level of that hospital building. She was certain she was pregnant and her dream of being a mother was coming true.

"I recommend you take the methotrexate injection again." Although he was aware of her history, he was confident that the same emergency would not happen again. "We are going to take a lunch break, take the time to think about your decision, and let me know after lunch."

Emilee went to a grassy area outside of the hospital to lay down and give herself time to contemplate what she must do. She could take the injection and risk it not functioning, leading to her tube bursting and emergency surgery, or opt for an immediate surgery, leaving her without fallopian tubes.

She called Beni with an update, and they discussed the options. She knew deep down that she should get the surgery, and made her final decision.

She headed back to the hospital and was admitted for immediate surgery.

Her doctor was there to greet her post operation. "You made the right decision; if you had not elected for the surgery the tube would have burst."

Although there was not a post-surgery examination, it was clear that the second fallopian tube was underdeveloped like the first had been.

Throughout this time of uncertainty, Emilee often drew from a Hawaiian-themed oracle deck for guidance. The card that continued to pop out for her was "Nalu," which translates to wave. A Hawaiian chant of "Ke Nalu Nei Ka Moana" was part of the explanation written about the card. A young man body-surfing a wave was the companion image. "The ocean is full of waves" the chant translated, and Emilee thought about how she could use this mantra during this difficult time.

She had just lost her last fallopian tube; chances of conceiving naturally were impossible. She had made that difficult decision on her own, and thankfully it had been the right one. Her man was thousands of miles away back in his own country, and here she was in the hospital bed pondering how she can move forward.

"This is my journey," she affirmed.

She had been through this difficulty before, and the heartbreak and physical pain she experienced were not foreign to her. She was capable of getting through this, and there must be a reason for it. She believed that she would not be dealt any cards in this life with more than she could handle.

She would find her lessons in this difficult time and understand that what she experienced happened because she chose it before she incarnated on this planet. She would learn to surf the waves of difficulty and uncertainty, and then move forward on her path. That is all she could do. The ocean does not stand still, it is an ever-flowing current, pulled by the tides and guided by the moon. She, too, was being guided; she was not separate from any of these natural phenomena.

Trauma Meditation

Everyone experiences hard times and trauma in their lifetime. It looks different for everyone, and we all process it in our own way.

Let's take a moment to think about a difficult event in our lives. Get into a comfortable seat or lie down. Feel free to record yourself reading through this text and play back for a complete relaxation experience.

Release the tension between your eyebrows and relax your jaw. Send awareness down your neck and across your shoulders. Feel the energy move down through your fingertips. Breathe into your ribcage and send the energy to your navel, hips and pelvis. Move the energy down through your knees to your ankles and toes. Relax completely and let go.

Allow thoughts to pass through your mind, not inviting them to stay. As you move towards deep relaxation, allow your body to feel weightless as if you are floating above the surface below you.

While keeping your body relaxed, begin to reflect on a time when you experienced a traumatic event. Think of a time that brought you heartache and emotional pain. What was this event?

(If this is too painful or triggering, please bring your awareness back to your breath and shift your awareness back to the present time. You do not have to move forward.)

Bringing this event to your consciousness, allow any emotions to surface surrounding the event. Breathe, and scan the body for physical sensations attached to these emotions.

Are you holding a muscle or body part tenser than the rest? Send your breath to that area and allow it to relax. Consider if you have healed from this event or if there is any work to do surrounding what happened.

Continue to breathe, taking as much time as you need, processing and revisiting what occurred.

- How did you overcome this event?
- What lessons can you take away from it?
- Has this event encouraged you to grow in any way?

Come back to your center and breathe into your body while noticing the present sensations.

What one word would you use to describe yourself during this event?

Send yourself compassion and love and anything you may feel you lacked from this experience.

If you would like to, offer yourself supportive touch. Rest one hand on your heart and the other on your lower abdomen. If another place on your body needs the support, honor that and move your hands there.

Feel your breath and the warmth of your body underneath you and send yourself love and compassion. Send compassion to anyone else/thing attached to this event. Think of a supportive word of encouragement you can offer yourself right now.

"I am_____." Say it outload three times.

Bring awareness back to your physical body. Wiggle your toes and your fingers, wet your lips with your tongue, and slowly come back into your body. Open your eyes when you are ready.

Write down this "I am" affirmation someplace you can read to yourself every day. You can write it on a post-it and hang it on your bathroom mirror, refrigerator, or dashboard of your car. Affirm to yourself daily that you are the one who can offer the most support to yourself.

If this opens up a wound for you, seek out further healing either through meditation or consulting with a therapist. You can even add this wish of healing to your Vison Board we will make later.

Chapter 12 – Rainbows

"Paradise has never been about places. It exists in moments. In connection. In flashes across time." ~ Victoria Erickson

"I WANT TO GET MARRIED IN A CASTLE!" Emilee chuckled to Beni on the phone.

She had recovered from her surgery and the two lovebirds communicated daily about their future together. Having saved a little money from her waitressing job, being in-between plans, and only having one suitcase worth of clothing in her possession, she was capable of relocating with him in Switzerland. It was only a matter of weeks until she was on her flight abroad.

Dressed in a full suit and tie, her Prince Charming awaited her at the airport. She was in awe as they drove by the lush green farmlands and through the Alps to the picturesque city where he lived in an apartment with his brother. She was fascinated by every feature of their European-style apartment, from the long steel door handles with a key that lived in the lock, to the toilet flush control installed in the wall. Everything seemed modern and well-thought out. Nothing about Switzerland was quickly thrown together or made from cheap plastic. The streets were immaculately clean, and everything seemed to run in perfect order. The old towns were well-preserved and multi-generational mountain huts were still occupied for family getaways in the mountains.

After the first night abroad and while still adjusting to the jet lag, the two went to Beni's parents' summer home located in the southern part of Switzerland bordered by Italy.

Wearing torn jeans and an old button-up shirt, she was very embarrassed to be dressed the way she was. She hardly owned more clothes than swimsuits coming from Maui. It was not like her old life in Wisconsin where she had different shoes for every day of the week, winter jackets, sweaters, and any accessory she needed. She had left this all behind, and because her life had been so transitory around the islands, she only owned what she could carry on an airplane.

The traditional greeting for the Swiss is three kisses on the cheek, left, right, and left. Not obeying this right away, Emilee greeted Beni's parents with a warm hug. They were very reserved at first, taking in this "American" who had won the heart of their youngest son.

"Show my mom your cards," Beni said to Emilee, encouraging her to give a tarot reading within the first 30 minutes of being in their home.

Because the language barrier was difficult at first, she hesitantly agreed that she would give his mom a reading. Feeling self-conscious, she gave his mother a Celtic cross reading, which revealed intimate details of his parents' past.

Feeling more comfortable and ready for an early sleep, the twosome retreated for the evening. The next day they would all go on their family boat around a great lake, taking in views of the Alps of southern Switzerland and the charming old cities of northern Italy. They took to a restaurant in a charming old city for lunch and ordered pizza. Emilee wasn't sure what was more surprising, that each person ordered an individual pizza or that they ate it with a fork and a knife.

She completely felt out of place with her worn leggings and old Hollister top while everyone was dressed so well. She tried her best to fit in with them, although being an American is something you cannot easily disguise while traveling in Europe.

The couple spent the next several weeks in the two-bedroom apartment that overlooked a small mountain and sat above a Pronto gas station.

Emilee's birthday was quickly approaching, and Beni was fast making plans for them to visit Paris. She was truly living an American girl's dream; a handsome European man with eyes only for her, traveling through southern Switzerland, Italy, and now Paris, France, for her birthday.

She had been rather vague on her Vision Board one year ago when she wrote "Travel Europe." She did not anticipate that her "Soulmate" would be from Europe, and he would whisk her away to his homeland and propose to her on her birthday in Paris, three short months after knowing her.

"Do you want to marry me?" Beni asked, with the symbolic black velvet box in his hand.

This was not a huge surprise; they had talked about marriage several times. It was the only way they could continue their union without being separated by oceans and continents. They both felt it was right, there weren't any doubts. Their relationship felt as if it always was, a connection that exceeded time and space.

She giggled with delight and squealed, "Yes!" as she took him down to the bed with a kiss.

They smooched and laughed as he offered her the engagement ring made from quartz crystal mined right from the Swiss Alps that surrounded the city they lived in. There could be no stone more meaningful or precious. She was not interested in a diamond; she could not fathom spending that amount of money on a ring when it could be spent on traveling to new places.

The wedding had to be planned quickly, as they wanted to marry before her visa expired so they could stay together in Switzerland. She had visualized herself in a white dress somewhere on a mountainside within enchanted castle walls, but she was going to choose a less extravagant wedding. They planned to marry in the Swiss equivalent of an American courthouse. She was not going to get a white wedding gown; she could not see how that was possible as their resources were not enough for a fancy dress and a wedding.

Her future mother-in-law took the couple to the city's bridal shop to look for a dress for Emilee. As they walked into the shop, a dress immediately grabbed Emilee's attention. It was a long white gown with sheer long sleeves and a flowery detail fit for a fairy.

"This is a dress from the fairies," she thought.

Knowing it was too much for her civil nuptials, she proceeded past the gown to look for a much less extravagant dress. With her future mother-in-law and the saleswoman working hard to find a dress like she had described, a heavy feeling grew in her stomach. None of these dresses sparked any joy inside of her. Impatience was growing from the women and sadness in Emilee.

Recognizing the uncomfortable energy, her fiancé pulled her aside and walked her to the extraordinary fairy dress hanging on the mannequin.

"You like this one, darling?" He had seen it as well and knew his future wife would love to wear it.

"Do you like this one?" his mother echoed.

"Yes," she replied, cautiously thinking she was foolish for even wanting such a dress.

"That won't fit you," the saleswoman alleged.

Emilee read the size on the tag and it was her size, so she asked to try it on. The gown was as comfortable as it was elegant. It slid on to her body as if it was placed in this shop specifically for her. It would not need alterations, it fit her perfect.

"We will take this!" Beni's mother said in her Swiss accent, "and now we have to have a party."

Emilee's face was warm with delight, but also uncertainty as she was receiving this beautiful and generous gift of a wedding gown. She grew excited for her wedding day, as it was turning out to be a great day for merriment.

They married legally first in the state building in the center of the old town and celebrated intimately in a public garden with champagne. Joined by a few friends and family, the newlyweds enjoyed a celebratory dinner. The extravagant celebration was set to take place two months later in a mountainside vineyard, with orchards and a beautiful view of the surrounding mountains.

On the day of the wedding celebration, the family got ready together in Beni's parents' home. His older brother, his grandmother, and his parents were there. His "Oma" cried when she saw Emilee in her gown. Excitement grew and gasps were heard as the bride walked down the stairs in her fairy gown, a wildflower crown adorned with greenery and pearls on her head, and an ornamental flower arrangement wrapped around her forearm. She was given a gift of Oma's pearl earrings, which she wore on both of her special wedding days.

The family headed together to a location unknown to Emilee for pre-party photographs. The anticipation grew inside her as they got near the photoshoot location; it was a Swiss Castle! Just as she had visualized it many times, her wearing a white gown next to her beloved, surrounded by castle walls in the mountains.

"This is Magic!" she thought.

How perfectly everything had fallen into place for them. His family was incredibly supportive of their matrimony. No one ever questioned their decision or suggested it was too soon to marry. Their love was recognized as honest and real and celebrated as such. Her father and stepmother were able to make the journey from Wisconsin and join the celebration.

As the family gathered around the grounds for photos, they took turns by groups and then the married couple together and individually. As Emilee was getting her photographs taken, she was guided to a small fountain in the garden. In the center of the fountain was a mermaid.

"How perfect," she thought, as she considered herself a mermaid who loved all things sea.

She felt surrounded by the fairies, the flowers, and all of the magic in the Universe. There were signs all around her that this was a special day, and this union was celebrated by the Universe.

Raindrops began to fall, and a brief moment of panic came over Emilee as her hair-sprayed hair became heavy with the moisture.

"There will be a rainbow." The thought rolled through her mind and she immediately became excited. She turned and screeched with delight.

Rainbows were her sign from the Universe that all is well, a glorious hello and reminder that she was well cared for in this life. She quickly grabbed her groom's hand and ushered the photographer to take a photograph of them with the colorful arch that painted the sky. Seemingly unexcited, the photographer began taking photos.

She did not mind that not everyone was excited as she, but this was one of the most thrilling moments of her life. Here she was, finally with her soulmate, in Europe, in a castle, in a beautiful wedding gown, and a magnificent rainbow was shining behind her. Hello, everyone... *This is what magic looks like.* It was the first rainbow she had seen in Switzerland. After months of living there she thought she would never see one. They were a near-daily occurrence in Hawai'i. This was a blessing.

The following day, while taking her father and stepmother on a tour, they encountered another magical rainbow. Two rainbows for two magical days of her father being with her, she concluded. He had been influential not only on her journey to Hawai'i, but in her ability to travel alone. His career that caused his constant travel also provided a lot of opportunity for Emilee to venture out to see him places. It was their bond that allowed her to be confident no matter where in the world she was.

A few weeks after the celebration, the couple was invited to Thailand for their honeymoon, and they joined her in-laws on a business-related trip. The couple enjoyed a private villa and had a marvelous time.

Emilee had "Travel to Thailand" written on the same Vision Board she included "Meet my Soulmate" and "Travel Europe."

She was pleasantly surprised with how her life was unfolding.

Manifestation: Ask and Receive

Acknowledge the blessings coming your way. It may be difficult to receive your blessings and allow them to flow freely to you. It's important to allow things to flow to you and be open to receiving.

Our job with manifesting is to ask for what we want, believe it will happen, feel worthy of receiving, and step out of the way when it comes to the delivery. It is not up to us to figure out the "how." That is why asking the Universe is often compared to the genie and the lamp.

- Make your wish: "Rub the lamp" by creating your Vision Boards. Speak your affirmations, and feel the gratitude in your heart.
- Continue to visualize, affirm, and be thankful while keeping your eye out for signs and confirmation.
- Acknowledge any work that may come up for you during these periods of waiting. The work will need to continue throughout your manifestations until you have healed that part of yourself, even after the manifestation has arrived. (More on doing the work in the following chapter.)
- Enjoy it when it arrives. Acknowledge that what you have asked for is surrounding you, and give thanks for all that has already manifested.
- Feel the joy in your heart for everything and every person that surrounds you. You are constantly manifesting your circumstances and experiences. Own up to your creational power!
- Avoid "must be nice" thoughts towards other people. Envy is a guide towards your own desires, and feeling jealous of others tells your subconscious that you cannot have what you want. Practice being happy for other people and what they have. This will come back to you.
- Avoid "would be nice" thoughts towards yourself. If you wish for something and then think it would be nice but it's not going to happen, this will prevent it from happening. Shift your "would be" to "will be" and spend time each day dreaming about it.

- Make necessary steps towards your goals. The Universe responds to your thoughts and actions. It may not deliver everything right to your doorstep, but it will extend you an energetic pathway to follow.

Chapter 13 – Work in Progress

"'Positive Vibes only' will only get you so far. The moment you sit with your 'negative' emotions and find what they are feeding on, the real work begins." ~ Instagram @ledbysource

THE NEWLYWED COUPLE continued to live in a shared apartment with her brother-in-law, which was often frequented by his girlfriend at the time. The brothers have had a tight relationship their entire lives. They knew everything about each other and have an unbreakable family bond.

It wasn't easy for the brother to accept a woman coming into his home and taking all of his younger brother's immediate attention. It was a big shift for him, but because of the love he had for his younger brother, he was supportive and never let any of his true feelings show.

Being highly sensitive and intuitive, Emilee knew that there was something difficult between herself and her new brother. They were very similar in personality, they both had a preference for one-on-one attention and the desire for sufficient alone time. They found this difficult to achieve while living together under one roof, and often competed for the attention of Beni.

It was exhausting for Emilee, and she struggled to be happy in her new Swiss life. The brother's girlfriend did not seem too interested in establishing a relationship with her. She was several years younger than Emilee, and wasn't very thrilled that the normalcy she knew with her boyfriend had been shaken by his brother meeting and marrying an American girl and the three of them living together.

Not having friends of her own, not speaking the language, and not being completely comfortable in the apartment left Emilee feeling slightly depressed in Switzerland. The plan was to move back to Hawai'i together, but they had to patiently wait for the Green Card process to finalize before they could move back to the States together.

She had manifested a true fairytale; a movie could be made about her life and it would end at the wedding in the Swiss castle back-dropped with a magic rainbow, and the couple lived happily ever after… which they did, but not without doing the work.

Emilee quickly realized that although her old patterns had seemingly disappeared while she was single and on her solo adventure, not so-desirable aspects of herself were surfacing once the couple began to settle. She felt insecure about herself living in this new foreign place. She was intimidated to venture out alone, and wanted to spend most of her time at home with her husband. She spent her time with him and his family, and sometimes hanging with him and his friends. She experienced jealousy, stemming from the fear of being abandoned if he was giving his attention elsewhere. She did not want to feel this way and was ashamed of herself for doing so. She could not understand how the work she thought she had done on herself had come undone. The darkness that she thought had left her when she became more positive was still inside her. She feared she was becoming the same person she previously was.

What separated this relationship from the rest and prevented her past cycles of rage and domestic violence from returning was her ability to recognize what was triggering her and openly discuss her feelings with her husband. When she felt angry, jealous, or insecure she would tell him how she was feeling, why she was feeling that way, and would express her desire not to feel that way.

He was always supportive and returned her concerns with a, "You are wonderful, Emmi-Boo."

Nothing she felt, thought, or said could turn him away. He loved her unconditionally and never judged her or called her irrational. He was truly patient and kind with her always. She also had to have forgiveness and understanding towards her emotions. She was more connected to herself as a woman and able to acknowledge the unhealed parts of her.

Emilee eventually ventured out and took a course in German. In her class she made a girlfriend from New Zealand, a fellow native English speaker. The girls bonded over their difficulties learning and speaking both German and the dialects of Swiss-German. They often went for coffee, and Emilee would invite her to do things while her spouse hung out with the guys. Switzerland became a lot more comfortable for her.

Over time, her relationship with her brother-in-law grew stronger and they would often bond over drinks, sharing their hearts and emotions with deep understanding and love for one another. Their mutual love for her husband was the foundation for their love and respect for each other.

The entire family quickly became like Emilee's own family. With her blonde hair and blue eyes, she looked like she was the daughter of her husband's mother.

Still experiencing undesirable emotions from time to time, Emilee was able to recognize that they didn't reflect who she truly was. She worked to forgive herself for not being positive and happy all of the time, and sometimes found it hard to suppress them. By acknowledging that the thoughts and emotions were not what she wanted to feel, and observing herself during times of upset, she was able to recover from the inner turmoil and work through it with her spouse.

It was through this kind of support the family provided that Emilee began to accept the shadow parts of herself and recognize them as the places that needed gentleness and compassion.

A few years later, while in therapy, Emilee put the pieces of her childhood experiences together and the patterns it created in her, for example, the fear of abandonment. Her mother was a foster parent from the time Emilee was seven, and cared for multiple kids, babysitting, well before that. Rarely having her mother to herself, and an open door of children cycling through her home left her feeling the need to receive as much intimate interaction as possible. Knowing this about herself has allowed her to be more forgiving with her inner child who longs to be seen and loved.

Grounding Techniques

The first nine years of our lives are the most impressionable. Situations and relationships during this time will influence our personalities, thoughts, and patterns for the rest of our lives. Through observing ourselves and our patterns, we may be able to break away from the cycles we have been in for so long.

It is okay to not always have positive thoughts and feelings. Although we want to avoid repetitive negative self-talk and judgements that prevent us from being in alignment with manifesting better things for ourselves, we want to honor our emotions and take time to process them. We want to be able to hold a safe space for each of our emotions to surface and observe them without judgement. It is okay to experience a bad day or even an off week, but come back from it.

Striving to be 100 percent positive all the time is not only unrealistic, it can be toxic in itself. That is where the term "toxic positivity" originates from. Each of our emotions are valid; allow them to surface, but do not let the ones that no longer serve you make a permanent home within you.

Ways to get grounded and come back to your center:

Journal your feelings: When you experience an upset, undesirable thought or emotion, or a confrontation, take time to process it through writing. Describe what happened and how you feel about the situation. Explore other times a similar experience has occurred. Become the observer of yourself in this situation and ask yourself what is triggering you.

It is not expected that you get to the root of all your issues without working with a licensed therapist, but these steps can help you become self-aware and practice forgiveness. We are all our younger selves carrying a shell of projections and experiences. Getting back to our true essence could be the most difficult and important work of our lives.

Practice Yoga: Looking at the philosophy of the 8-limbed path of Yoga, we understand that physical Yoga only accounts for 1/8th of the practice. Going inward and observing ourselves through self-study will lead us on a journey of awareness where we can become the observer of our actions, our thoughts, and recognize our patterns. We can begin to let go of attachment to certain ideas and emotions, which will allow us to break out of certain patterns that have developed over time. Separating this baggage from our true essence, which is our light body, will help us remember our truth and connect to our core values.

Create a daily practice of moving your body, sit quietly while you observe your thoughts in meditation, and write about your experiences in your journal. Begin to see yourself from an outside perspective without judgement. Imagine if you were looking back at your younger self and your younger self was dealing with the current situation. Send your younger self unconditional love and empathy. Be the one who gives you what you need so you can move forward and attract new experiences in your life.

Go outside and spend time in nature. Put your bare feet on the ground and connect to the vibrations of the earth. Eat nourishing foods made from fresh ingredients. Indulge in self-care. Rest if needed.

Chapter 14 – The Embryo

"You can't fake it with the Universe. You can't pretend to be kind, loving and positive; your vibration will suggest otherwise -- and the Universe will match your frequency. Take care of yourself internally and your life will change externally, for the better."
~ Unknown

AFTER A YEAR AND A HALF of living abroad, the couple moved back to Hawai'i together. Just like the first time Emilee had ventured to the islands, her father was working on O'ahu again. They began their joint journey in Honolulu, thinking it would be the best place for them to find work opportunities.

During the few months they were on O'ahu they visited Maui for a week. While visiting the Valley Isle, it felt more like home to them and they decided to make their move back to that island. They both found jobs right away and rented a small cottage on the North Shore. Everything quickly fell into place for them.

Beni's biggest dream was to join the U.S. Military. Emilee discovered this dream during one of their first evenings together. She passionately demanded that he admit what his dream of all dreams was.

"I want to be a Navy Seal," he said nervously.

"You can do it!" she yelled with enthusiasm.

Getting him into the U.S. Military was always the goal for the couple. After hearing him admit his desire, she felt a deep sense of purpose to help him achieve his goal. She had been so fearless herself, moving to the islands and following her dreams, she was destined to encourage this soul to do the same. He needed her to achieve this.

They had made a Vision Board together in Switzerland. They divided the board in half; the left being feminine for her and the right and masculine side for him. In the center they placed what they wanted to achieve together, and on their sides, they placed their individual wishes. His side was highly emphasized with images of the military. Hers was centered around writing books and creating a wellness center. In the middle they highlighted growing their family and owning their dream home.

After a year of living back on Maui, the couple was ready to pursue their biggest dreams; he joined the military and Emilee was going to get pregnant. Without fallopian tubes, her only option for conception was in vitro fertilization. Stubbornly, she refused to believe that this was her only option. She was magical, dammit! She surely could get pregnant naturally, write a book about it, and meet Oprah! That was her plan and she was immovable on it.

An opportunity to join a Vision Board workshop surfaced, and being curious about what else there was to learn about manifesting, Emilee joined the group. The workshop was stretched over four weekends, a few hours each Saturday for one month.

The class began with accessing the group's deepest desires and then writing them out on paper in present tense with positive emotions attached.

"I am joyously pregnant naturally," she wrote as her number one goal.

The host of the workshop suggested that Emilee should write, "I am pregnant with grace and ease."

It took some convincing, but she reluctantly made the edit. She visualized herself conceiving gracefully and with ease. She chose a picture of a pregnant belly with a pink t-shirt to represent her pregnancy.

On this Vision Board she put where she wanted them to be located once her husband joined the military. Beni had chosen to enlist in the U.S. Army, and his MOS was a Cavalry Scout. Colorado was the location that called to her the most. She cut out magazine images of the snowcapped mountains, elk, and a happy couple wrapped in a warm flannel blanket snuggled outside somewhere cold.

During his time away in basic training she spent her days dreaming about their happy military life in Colorado, and her getting pregnant with grace and ease.

After the long weeks away at AIT training, he called her to say he received his duty station orders. "El Paso, Texas," he reported to her on FaceTime.

"NO!" she wailed, as she did not want to go to Texas, she wanted to go to Colorado.

They hung up the phone, both feeling disappointed and a little unsure about what their lives would be like in Texas. It did not feel right to her, she had planned on living near the Rockies. She spent that evening in conflict, focusing all of her energy on a change in the orders.

The next day she received another call from her husband, "My orders have changed! We are going to Fort Carson!"

Excitement rained over the couple as their vision of their future in the military and on the mainland was coming to fruition. Emilee knew if she was powerful enough to change military orders, she could do anything.

Once settled in their new rental apartment outside the gates of Fort Carson, Emilee established health care to discuss fertility treatments. Because of her dual tubal removal, there were not any waiting requirements, she could move ahead with the in vitro process immediately. She was given a referral to an IVF clinic and began the procedure within the first few months of living there.

Planning her cycle around her husband's training schedule, she chose to have a January egg retrieval. The stimulation cycle produced 6 eggs, 3 were fertilized, and 1 embryo developed into a blastocyst. After the genetic testing results were complete, the couple knew that the embryo was a little girl and she had tested normal.

Excitement surrounded the two as they knew they had a baby embryo frozen and waiting to be transferred. A 9-month deployment was approaching in February, so the couple decided to wait until after Beni left to make the transfer. This would mean he would return in time to see his daughter born. This would also leave Emilee on her own for the entire pregnancy. Separately, they would both be experiencing their biggest wishes coming true, linked by the support of the other.

Once again, the two would be separated by countries with the hope of pregnancy between them.

In the weeks prior to her frozen embryo transfer, Emilee kept herself busy. She worked as an assistant for a chiropractor and made friends with her fellow employees. One of them, a Colorado native, took her on a shopping tour in the "Old City." They ventured into an apothecary which housed hand-crafted flower essences. The essences were healing on a vibrational level.

"Do you have anything for infertility?" she asked the friendly shop owner.

The woman smiled and directed her towards a special blend that would be helpful for implantation. "You have the soul of a baby girl with you," the woman stated tenderly.

Alertness rose up through Emilee's body as she became overwhelmed with excitement at this confirmation. She knew this pregnancy would take; it had been so easy up to this point, and magical messengers like this woman were confirmation that her daughter was with her, ready to incarnate.

In March, the hormone therapy resumed priming Emilee's body to receive the transfer of her one surviving embryo. Excited for this magical event, she bought her baby embryo flowers and wrote out a welcome card for her. She had an image of her embryo printed out, which she admired as much as any woman who sees their first ultrasound. It was unique to be in love with a cluster of cells seen only from under a microscope.

She arranged for a friend to drive her home after the transfer. With two amethyst crystals in her pocket as suggested by the apothecary shop owner, she nervously laid back on the operating table. She was alert yet relaxed with the valium she was prescribed for the procedure. She watched on the screen as the doctor placed her baby girl inside of her uterus. She recorded the event for her husband to watch afterwards, and everyone cheered as they watched the catheter place the embryo perfectly inside her uterus. It was truly a magical moment.

In vitro seemed so unnatural to her in the beginning, yet each step of the experience proved to hold an element of magic. She considered herself spoiled from the process and the intimacy of knowing her embryo's gender before even becoming pregnant. It was actually quite thrilling.

On the drive home from her transfer, her friend went through a fast-food drive through to get Emilee a large French fry. It was a sworn method written all over online platforms that French fries were the key to the embryo sticking. She enjoyed a large fry and a strawberry milkshake, and cozied up on her heating pad once at home. She spent the next few days alone, eating warming foods, heated pineapple, and spiced teas.

On the day of possible implantation, the lilies bloomed in the bouquet she had bought to welcome her baby girl. She felt slight cramping and her face began to glow within the next few days. She also began to run slightly warmer. All of her symptoms pointed to a successful transfer.

Testing at home was discouraged as it could provide a false negative, but she wanted her spouse to receive the good news at the same time as she would. She decided to test at home on day 9 after the transfer. With Beni on FaceTime, she took the test and left it in the bathroom while they waited. She sat on the foot of the bed in the next room and nervously passed the next few minutes talking with her husband. As she walked back to the test, her heart nearly jumped from her chest as she saw the one obvious dark pink line from across the room. As she moved closer to the stick, she could see the second line was faintly there as well.

It was positive! She did it! They did it! The in vitro had worked and she was pregnant with grace and ease.

After week 9 of her pregnancy, and once the heartbeat was established, she moved back to Maui for the remainder of her pregnancy. She desired to be near the ocean and in the healthy atmosphere that living in Hawai'i offers. She lived alone in a cottage and sought care from a midwife friend.

During week 14 of the pregnancy, Emilee experienced sudden bleeding. An alarming-sized puddle of blood pooled underneath her as she laid in her bed. Frightened, she ran to the toilet and more red liquid came out. Panicked, she called her midwife and was instructed to call an ambulance.

"I am so sorry," her midwife apologized for the possible loss.

"Am I losing my baby?" She cried and trembled as she waited for the ambulance to arrive.

Calmness overcame her and she focused on controlling her emotions. Whatever came she could handle, she knew that.

As she lay reclined on the stretcher, a rainbow appeared through the rear window of the ambulance. Relief washed her worries away as the comfort of her trusted rainbow assured her that all is was it should be.

"You're very calm," the EMT said, surprised at Emilee's ability to stay relaxed for the ride.

She spent the 30-minute drive to the hospital watching the rainbow as it danced across the entire island and saw to it that she arrived good and well to the hospital.

An ultrasound diagnosed a subchorionic hematoma, an opening where blood was coming out of her uterus. Her baby girl was healthy and unharmed, and the hematoma went on to heal on its own around week 19.

Determined to have an unmedicated home birth once her husband returned from deployment, Emilee proceeded with her at-home care with her midwife, who she had met two years prior when she took an Introduction to Midwifery course on Maui. During the final day of the training, the midwifery students celebrated the program completion on the beach. A labyrinth was drawn in the sand for each of them to walk through. When Emilee arrived in the center of the maze, she hopped over the edge and exited without fully completing it. Knowing the story of her previous pregnancy losses, the midwife gently guided her to walk back in, carefully touched her shoulders from behind and walked her all the way through and back out again. All of the women watched in silence, holding space for the intention that one day Emilee would complete a full-term pregnancy and birth of her rainbow baby.

Her husband was released from deployment just in time for the due date, and was able to join her on Maui for the birth of their daughter, Ellee Moon. Emilee succeeded in birthing at home after a 3-day long intense labor journey. She survived a hemorrhage that required emergency surgery and an overnight stay at the hospital, separating her from her newborn for the first night.

The family of three went back to Colorado to finish out the military contract for another year, and then moved back to Maui, where they are actively creating the next part of their journey and working towards another cycle of IVF.

Faith and Flexibility

There are many events that will happen in our lives that are out of our control. Pregnancy and birth are always unpredictable, and I had to surrender to both the process of conception and of labor. I wanted more than anything to get pregnant naturally without fallopian tubes. I have read stories about it happening, and was positive that I could make it happen with visualization.

The Universe does not respond to childlike demands, it rewards empowered commands. Trying to tell the Universe that I will conceive naturally is telling it how to do its job. But it is not our place to micromanage how the events will unfold for us. Affirming that I would conceive with grace and ease allowed room for the Universe to decide the "how" and allow all of the lines of energy to fall into place for the desire to manifest.

How I conceived was out of my control. Although I wanted it to happen magically so that Oprah would find my story inspiring, that was not how it was meant to happen for me. Once I surrendered to the possibility of conceiving with IVF, I was able to see the signs and follow the guidance from the Universe. I knew that I was going to have a baby, and I received confirmation from the Universe through messages from strangers and gut feelings. I spent lots of time in meditation communicating with Ellee's soul, and I knew that she was coming to join me on this planet.

This is why I continued to have faith when I experienced bleeding, and felt the encouragement from the rainbow in the back of the ambulance.

I imagined my birth going as easy as could be with my high tolerance for pain. During the last few weeks of pregnancy I did feel that something was going to happen with the placenta. I asked my midwife multiple times about a retained placenta and hemorrhaging. When I was being transferred to the hospital after giving birth, I rode in the backseat of the truck as calm as could be. As I felt that this would happen, there was not much I could do but seek treatment. I had opted for a homebirth so I could avoid unnecessary medical intervention and not be separated from my newborn. Instead, I received necessary medical care and a full night away from her.

All the planning in the world could not have forced the birth to go the way I wanted it to.

We have to remain flexible with the process, surrender in faith, and move forward with optimism. That does not mean there are not stored emotions around all of it. We are allowed to feel discouraged, heartbroken, and defeated throughout the process. Allow any feelings to come up to the surface, and then work towards moving forward.

We're going to make our Vision Boards in the next chapter. While looking for images and uncovering your desires, avoid letting the "how" prevent you from believing you can have these things and experiences.

Chapter 15 – Creating a Vision Board

"You've always had the power, my dear. You just had to learn it for yourself." ~ The Wizard of Oz

WHAT IF THE LIFE YOU DESIRE is really just a thought away? Could your dreams come true by simply writing down affirmations and gluing magazine photos to a piece of poster board? Is the Universe always responding to your vibrations and daydreams? Are you, in fact, responsible for the very circumstances surrounding you?

These are all questions that may be going through your mind while you read through these pages.

"She must have luck to marry a wealthy guy from Switzerland and have all of her dreams come true," may be something you smirked to yourself when reading my stories.

I have heard several reasons as to why things happened for me that do not include the choices I've made and the work I've done on myself to attract the life I have. The truth is, every single decision I have made has placed me exactly where I am today.

Perhaps my traumas and lessons seem lesser than your own or perhaps you can completely relate. All of our journeys will hold their own fate, lessons, and trauma. It is not up to us to discredit another's work and growth as they move along their path.

"There are many paths to the top of the mountain, but the view is always the same." ~ Chinese Proverb

What I would like you to take away from this book is a belief in yourself and your ability to create the life you deserve. We are all equally capable and entitled to this creative magic, but it doesn't come without doing the work. We have to take an honest look at our thoughts and beliefs about ourselves, judgements we have towards ourselves and others, our behavioral patterns, emotional wellbeing, and the purity of our heart. The Universe responds to your vibrational frequency. Making your vibration higher through joy, love, and compassion will help you manifest better outcomes for yourself.

The Universe always says, "Yes!"

It is up to you to grab onto that line of energy it sends by way of noticing the signs, messages, and synchronicities. It is up to you to heal the parts of yourself that prevent you from flourishing.

This work can be life-long and take assistance from licensed professionals. It is up to you to take care of yourself, eat well, practice deep relaxation, and physically move your body. Heighten your intuition by keeping your body free of harsh chemicals and toxins and honoring your body's cyclical rhythms. Rest when you need, and create when you feel inspired. It's not selfish to fill your own cup first, in fact, it's the most generous thing you can do for others. The fuller your own cup, the more you have to give to others.

Stay true to your core values and honor your inner child. You are not separate from who you were at birth. Allow yourself to join forces with your inner child to emphasize your passions and abilities. You have been you all along, but you have been carrying around others' baggage which has helped to form your reality. It is time to let that shit go because it does not belong where you are going. You are on a journey towards healing. If you are a parent, consider how your traumas and patterns are influencing your own children or even your children's children. The changes you make in yourself influence everyone around you. When you heal yourself, you heal your family line, forward and behind.

Work through the exercises throughout the book as often as you like. Give yourself a monthly check-in of your health, relationships, spiritual connection, career, home, and money. Keep yourself accountable through journaling and self-study. Take an honest look at yourself and do not be afraid to dive in deep. If at any time you think you would like support, reach out to a local therapist. Therapy can be transformative, therapists need therapists. Normalize going to therapy and talking about your wounds with your close circle. Address family traumas if it feels safe for you, and practice forgiveness from your end.

Focus all of your work inward. You cannot do this work for anyone, nor can you force them to do it for themselves. When you see yourself as the wounded child, your perception of others may change. You may see the patterns of your family members or friends as a result of their own childhood. Listen to their childhood stories; it will help you understand from a place of empathy and compassion. This does not mean that you have to accept someone's behavior if it does not feel right to you. It means that you are understanding and compassionate towards their own healing journey. This can be done from a distance. Not everyone will leave this earth healed. Many will take their hurt and bitterness with them to the grave.

It's my belief that whatever we do not learn in this lifetime will be waiting for us in the next.

Make Vision Boards and practice visualization exercises. Look at the world with child-like wonder and trust that the Universe will provide for you.

On behalf of the Native Hawaiian population, I would like to say that I am *not* encouraging every person who reads this book to up and move to Hawai'i, but I *do* encourage you to find your own dream. Listen to the calling of your soul and go on a wild journey. You also don't have to be vegan to have success with this; follow the passions and purpose that are deep within you. Have the courage to take a leap of faith. When you make a change, the Universe responds with more of the change you wish to see.

You may be already settled with a partner and have children. Your goal doesn't have to be to move away and start over, but do not limit yourself because you have a family. Co-create a shift together that will benefit everyone.

Be of service to the world around you. Acknowledge your impact on the planet and its inhabitants, and do your best to come from a place of love. If you ever feel undeserving of manifesting something great, give back, volunteer, or donate. Create a balance of giving and receiving so that you feel worthy of receiving your desires.

Change your thought process from "I can't," to "I am!" Be genuinely happy for others. Replace "must be nice," with "I am happy for you!"

See yourself as the attractor and acknowledge that life is working with you and not happening to you. Trust in yourself. Love yourself. I am very excited for the way your life will unfold.

Let's get to work creating our Vision Boards!

Begin gathering the supplies for your Vision Board. You can start to gather things you have around your house or put together a shopping list. Have a pair of scissors on hand, a glue stick, markers, paint, or anything you would like to decorate with. You may want to have a storage container to keep your supplies and magazine clippings together as you work on your board.

There are several types of Vision Boards you can make. Consider where you will place your board, what works best for your living space, and where you will see your board the most.

Choose your medium:

- Poster Board: Purchase a poster board in the size you would like your board to be.
- Corkboard: Choose your corkboard and have pushpins on hand.
- Binder: Have a three-ring binder with sheet protectors and pages to decorate and insert.
- Notebook: Buy or find a notebook that you would like to use.
- Post-its: Use any you have around or purchase new.
- Word Document: Have a document creator on your computer.
- Phone: Download a collage photo maker on your phone. (You can also take photos of any of the above media and create a digital version for your phone.)

Upcycle tip: You can use any binders or boards you have around the house. I have used an old canvas painting and painted it white and used this as the base of my Vision Board. Feel free to get creative and turn anything you would like into a board and place where you can see it every day to visualize your desires. There is no wrong way to create one.

If you are creating a physical board, begin gathering magazines. You can check libraries or businesses; people are often tossing old magazines. If searching for a specific style of magazine, purchase it from a bookstore or grocery store. You may also search for images and words online and print them out. If you are going digital, begin collecting images and words and saving them into a folder on your phone or computer.

Choose any images that resonate with you. They can be of your dream vacation, your ideal partner, a house, a car, or activity. Chosen images can be of your favorite food or a colorful image that contains soothing colors. If you have a partner or a family, you may choose images of families doing things together. You may also use actual photos of yourself doing the activities you want to do more of. Any image or word that calls to your soul, save it and put it into your collection.

I will often have magazine images of colors or designs that I'm attracted to. The colors I choose are soothing to my soul and immediately draw me into my center when I look at them.

Any image that calls to your higher self, go ahead and choose it. Every image does not have to be something you are trying to manifest physically. It can be a representation of you and connection to a higher power or your higher self. As you put together your collage, these images make the board visually appealing and stimulating to you. Your images should leave you feeling grounded and at peace.

Choose words as affirmations and mantras. Use words that you find empowering, words that tell the story of your dreams and of the emotions you will feel once you have it. Tying positive emotions to your images is important, as you do not want to manifest your dream home and then be absolutely miserable in it. You want to feel joy and gratitude for your desires.

Find a comfortable place to work. You may also choose to create a joint Vision Board with your spouse or as a group exercise with your friends. Get grounded and begin by setting your intentions for the experience. You may want to smudge yourself, draw oracle cards, burn incense, or have a ceremonial beverage like tea. Let this experience be a celebration of your dreams and your creational power.

Have your list of what you would like to manifest and focus on at this time. These can be physical things, personal areas of growth, and opportunities. Have your positive affirmations written about how you will feel when you manifest these items on your list. You may also do this part after you have created your board. If you are feeling stuck and uncertain about what you want to manifest, allow yourself to be inspired by the images you find. Allow the Vision Board to flow through you.

If you have not already collected all of your photographs, begin flipping through magazines or browsing online. Either print off the photographs or download the images, depending on your medium. Choose images that spark joy and call to your core values. If something speaks to you and you don't know why, go for it, the meaning will reveal itself in time.

- **Poster/Cork Board**: Once you have all your images ready, you may want to organize them on the board before securing with glue or push pins. I like to start gluing and let the design unfold like artwork. How you arrange the board is individual. You may begin by placing images that represent you and your core values at the center and place your desires around you. You may use an image of yourself as well to help you visualize yourself manifesting your desires. You may also scatter everything throughout the design, so it is without a center focal point.
- **Binder/Notebook**: Similar to the poster board, you will arrange images for gluing. I like to divide the pages by categories. The first page(s) represent myself and what makes me joyful. I may cut out something from a magazine that says, "I am so happy with who I am," any statement or quote that defines me. Then I would proceed to create a page for the individual topics I would like to manifest. Here are a few examples:

- o Travel
- o Career
- o Love Life
- o Spirituality
- o Growth
- o Self-Care
- o Enjoyment
- o Dream House
- o Dream Bathroom/Kitchen
- o Gratitude

I recently weaned my toddler from breastfeeding. It was an extremely intimidating task for me to begin, but after I created a page for my breastfeeding/weaning journey and attached my weaning affirmations, it happened with ease.

- **Digital Collage/Word Document**: Have all of your chosen images and words saved in a folder. Using a collage creator, place your images together. If you have more images than spaces, make several collages. For the documents, arrange the images and words like you would on a physical board; allow your creativity to shine. With either method, you can print it out and save it to your phone.
- **Post-it notes**: Post-its can be used alongside your other visualization methods or on their own. You can write down mantras, affirmations, and desired outcomes on them. Place them on or near your existing Vision Board or use them individually. Place them in everyday places like near your computer, inside your vehicle, on your bathroom mirror, where you hang your car keys, and near your bed.

It is important to revisit your Vision Board as much as possible and spend time daily focusing on your visualizations while saying your gratitude affirmations. I have tried several methods of daily viewing and have had success with all of them. Choose the best method for your routine and living space. If you've created a poster/cork board, hang this somewhere in your living space where you will see it multiple times a day. You may take photos of the board with your phone and print off these images and hang in other locations throughout the home.

Another option is to place the Post-its affirmations accompanying your board throughout your home to remind you to visualize. Store your binder/notebook next to your bed or keep it near throughout the day. It is easy to tuck this away and not look at it. Make it part of your daily routine to flip through the pages. You may also choose to remove a page from the binder and carry it with you throughout the day. Print your collage/word document and place it in the places of your choosing. Save individual images or images of the entire board on the home screen of your electronic devices.

Take time to look at your Vision Board daily. Take a few minutes to imagine yourself through your own senses experiencing these desires. Use all of your senses and visualize as many details as possible. Incorporate experiencing positive emotions to these manifestations, imagining the joy you will feel in your relationship, the happiness your new car brings you, and the warmth and comfort of your new home.

Remember not to focus on what you do not want more of, and you cannot tell the Universe in which way these things will manifest.

Your job with manifestation is to:

1. Ask for what you want.
2. Create a Vision Board.
3. Practice visualization daily.
4. Pay attention to signs and messages.
5. Take action towards your goals.
6. Believe that you can achieve your desires and that you deserve them.
7. Self-study, journaling, and meditation.
8. Practice gratitude.
9. Work on your healing.
10. Raise your vibration.

Happy Vision Boarding!

Chapter 16 – Realistic Expectations

"All things are difficult before they are easy." ~ Unknown

WHILE THIS BOOK was in its editing stages, I was undergoing a second round of IVF. I feel that sharing my story surrounding the experience is essential to the teachings in the book. I want you to believe in magic, and your personal power, but I would also like you to understand that the tools in this book will not make you invincible to painful experiences.

The last year of the lockdown has been a year full of unknowns. It has been a year full of "whys."

My husband and I made the decision to extend our family and undergo another round of in vitro fertilization. It was always the goal to have two children, hopefully a son to join our now two-year-old daughter Ellee Moon. As I mentioned previously, I was very blessed with the success of my first IVF cycle.

I explored the option of a second cycle when Ellee was 14 months old. Still breastfeeding, I decided to wait until she was weaned. After she turned two, I was ready to begin weaning and prepare for the fertility treatments. I also mentioned previously that I made a weaning Vision Board and it ended up being a gentler process that I could have hoped for. It has been months since weaning and I continue to wear bandages over my nipples to distract her from wanting to suckle. At night and early morning, she will find my breasts and still lay her sweet pink cheeks upon them.

My heart breaks knowing that I gave up this special bond and nourishing routine for a "maybe" child. Even though I was ready to wean, and I hadn't slept a full night in the entirety of her existence, I still cry every time she wants to be soothed by them. I was grateful the weaning happened quickly and without a fight so that I could proceed with my fertility treatment plan.

The doctor and I met several times over the last year, both in person and over an online portal. There was a synchronicity in his name; it rhymed with the previous doctor's name who had cared for me during my first cycle. I took that as a sign it was meant to be.

Going through IVF a second time was more nerve-wrecking. Now, I had a daughter to think about in regard to choices that could affect my long-term health, as well as the possible dangers that come with surgery and undergoing anesthesia.

The treatment center is on the island of O'ahu, which requires a short flight for each visit. During my cycle, I would need to fly there a total of four times, and my husband would need to join for two of those. Flying during a pandemic poses its own challenges, and thankfully providing a doctor's note would exempt us from a mandatory test or 10-day quarantine. Airlines mandate that two-year-olds must also wear masks during flights, which we had practiced with Ellee many times. We were confident it wouldn't be a problem.

Preparing my body the best I knew how, I refrained from alcohol, caffeine, and ate only gluten-free and plant-based foods for months prior to the retrieval. Feeling the need to withdraw from the outside world, I kept my socialization and online presence to a minimum.

I also took the time to create a new Vision Board, which included my upcoming pregnancy with the same affirmation as last time, "I am pregnant with grace and ease," and I added, "I am pregnant when the time is right."

I also created a digital collage of things I wanted to manifest, including writing this book, creating my oracle cards, and a few other goals I am working towards. I saved the image to my home screen and printed it out to hang on my refrigerator as well as next to my bed.

On the first flight to O'ahu, we traveled together for the baseline appointment. Ellee refused to wear her mask on the airplane, and we were grateful no one gave us any trouble about it.

During the appointment, Beni and I both received blood work and were given a cooler bag of medications and the supplies needed to administer them. I was overwhelmed as I sat listening to the nurse instruct me how to mix each medication, measuring liquids and injecting them into powder medications before drawing them up into the syringe and injecting into my belly. Although I had gone through it all before, it was well before I had "mom brain" and a toddler distracting me from the instruction. I left the appointment feeling somewhat confident I would be able to navigate all of the instructions.

The first few nights of the stimulation cycle only required a medicated patch on my shoulder; nothing to mess up there. When it came time for injections, nerves took over as I began unpacking all of the medical supplies I had been given. Reflecting back on the instructions, I searched for a specific cap that could be placed on the saline mixture to draw up the liquid needed to inject it effortlessly into the powder. This cap was crucial to mixing the multiple medications with ease. I began to panic when I realized they had been left out of my supply bag. Would this affect my cycle? Could I mix my medications now? Stress took over my body as I called the office for support. We were able to sort out that I could use the small needles I was given to draw up medications, it would just take a bit longer than with the caps.

I felt relieved to begin my cycle, but with slight mistrust in my clinic. I would easily forgive the small human errors if my cycle was successful, but I knew that if it wasn't, I would find myself questioning what else they may have overlooked. The previous clinic I used had its share of mistakes, but because I was successful in conceiving, these things have been long forgotten.

The rest of the cycle seemed to go smooth as I continued with my injections. I was able to acquire the caps I needed after my first solo trip to the other island and clinic. After two visits on my own and promising lab results, I received the date for my retrieval. I booked flights and a hotel for my family. We stayed directly on Waikiki beach. The same Duke's restaurant I went to in my earlier O'ahu years was located in the lobby of the hotel.

I specifically wanted to be near my old stomping grounds where so much of my journey had unfolded. I spent dozens of evenings watching sunsets and sending my wishes to the Universe right on the very beach that surrounded the hotel. It was there I visualized my move to Maui long before I had even touched foot on the island. It was also there that I dreamed the most about meeting my soulmate and having children. How magical to bring them both back to the very place where our reality was visualized!

Because of travel restrictions and mandatory quarantine rules, we could only spend one night on the island. This meant that we had to fly home after my surgery, otherwise we would need a negative Covid test or we would need to quarantine when we returned to Maui. My mother was coming to visit after my surgery, and to avoid disruption of her travel plans, flying home the same day was the easiest option.

We enjoyed a family lunch at Duke's and took a swim in the crowded ocean. I grabbed a blue spirulina smoothie after the beach, blue for our future son. The blue theme was painted on my toes, as I chose the color thinking of a successful boy embryo. Beni and I had fantasized about having a son. We named him Benjamin Luca Kern, Jr. He was as real as any of us. My intuitive friends all commented that they felt a boy was coming. It felt as if it already was. There was no doubt that the cycle would be successful.

Although I felt confident that the cycle would be successful, I experienced guilt over how lucky I would be with having two easy and successful IVF cycles. It almost wouldn't be fair. But I justified my future success with the fact that I had already experienced loss twice, and I wouldn't have to go through that lesson and sadness again. I also decided that because I shared so openly about my last cycle, I would keep quiet this round.

The night before my surgery, we ordered food to our room from a nearby restaurant. We cuddled together in the comfortable hotel bed and felt very optimistic. Bright and early we rose and drove to the clinic to retrieve my eggs and create our future baby.

In my hairnet and hospital gown, I laid in the recovery room bed awaiting my treatment. I chatted with the nurse as she attempted to place my IV. After a second try, I was attached to liquids and headed back to the surgical room. As the anesthesia kicked in, I felt weightless as I heard the staff conversing about buffalo chicken wings while I drifted off to sleep.

"I'm so happy with your staff," I remember slurring as I awoke from surgery.

After I recovered, Beni and Ellee escorted me out of the clinic. We drove back to the hotel to gather our things before our short flight home. We decided it was easier to have me run in alone and for Beni to circle around and come back over the only option of valet parking.

As I hurried through the lobby, a concerned hotel employee asked if I was okay. I assured him I was and assumed because I had both arms taped up from IV attempts, I appeared in slight distress. A woman stared at me the entire elevator ride up to my floor as if I were an oddity. When I entered my room and noticed myself in the mirror, I realized the clinic had left monitor stickers on my chest. I may have very well looked like an escaped hospital patient, especially alarming during a pandemic. I had a good laugh at myself, removed all bandaging, and headed back to the lobby for my pickup.

We headed back to Maui and I went right to rest upon returning home. My mother arrived two days after my surgery to help with Ellee while I recovered.

Within days I knew that my retrieval produced 12 eggs, 10 of which were fertilized. Three of those eggs grew to a 5-day blastocyst and were biopsied and tested for genetic abnormalities. It would be at least two weeks before we knew the genders and chromosomal status of the embryos.

We enjoyed the week of my mother's visit. She had time to bond with her granddaughter whom she rarely gets to see. The follow up with my doctor was a few days after her departure.

During the routine video call, not expecting to have an update about the 3 embryos, Beni and I excitedly took the call.

"There's some bad news" the doctor said first.

Immediately I thought my 3 embryos dropped down to 2, but that was expected with this cycle.

"All of your embryos tested abnormal."

A short laugh exited my throat as I digested what he had just told us. *"All of the embryos are abnormal,"* I repeated to myself, as if I hadn't heard it clear the first time.

The moments that followed were filled with the doctor talking and me not being able to listen. I responded that I was unable to digest anything in that moment, and I would contact the clinic when I could gather my thoughts. I was in shock. It was not the outcome I could have imagined for our embryos. Completely unexpected, I was unable to immediately process the information. I began to cry shortly before the video call ended.

Once the laptop was closed, I wailed the cry of a mother who had just lost her children. The sobs that came out of my throat I had never released before, although the pain was all too familiar. My husband held me as I crumbled and my heart shattered into pieces.

The update hit us both hard, and the rest of the day was difficult for us. We had dropped a vehicle off for service that morning, so we headed to town to pick it up. I asked Beni if I could drive home alone and that he drive back with Ellee.

Alone, I drove back towards home, hoping for a sign from the Universe. I needed a message as I scrolled through the radio for the entire 30-minute drive, hoping for a favorite song or anything to sooth my soul. Nothing played that resonated. I saw the moon high in the afternoon sky and I was irate with it. I did not care to see the moon. The clock turned to 4:44 and it made me angry, I hated my favorite synchronistic numbers in that moment. I was furious with the Universe, I was completely confused and wanted to know why!?

Because I had been so quiet on social media the months prior, I decided to do what I know best when it comes to my grief. I shared my story. I had documented my IVF journey with photographs on my phone. I wrote the story of what happened and shared a few images from the treatment and of our family traveling to O'ahu. The response I received was heartwarming. My family and friends wishing me well allowed me to process my grief further. Each comment and private message allowed more tears to surface that may have otherwise been tucked away, hidden under strength. I needed to process my grief as it existed in different forms: sadness, anger, shock, and disbelief.

When I share my vulnerability on social media, I open a doorway for others to share their own painful experiences. I received private messages from women I knew distantly who were also struggling with IVF. They know my pain all too well and wanted me to know I'm not alone. They are grateful that I shared my story, and I am grateful that they have the courage to reach out and connect with me. An invisible bond forms and my strength rebuilds as I remember part of my purpose again.

I know the answers to why this happened the way it did will never come from an outside source. Because it was a chromosomal abnormality, they do not have an answer for us. The reason has to unfold over time, and one day I know I will understand and be grateful for the way things happened.

It's hard to hear these words coming from other people who are trying to help you grieve. The last thing I wanted to hear was "God has a plan," or "At least you are blessed with the daughter you already have."

I wanted to know why the hell I just put my body through all of that and it was unsuccessful. I had done everything I could on my end, as well as practiced the tools I write about in this book, yet the outcome was not what I had wished for. What a tough pill for me to swallow.

I will say I have a deep sense of gratitude for the outcome because I get to come back to my readers with more to my story. It is important that I do not lead you down a path of certainty that things will work out exactly the way you wanted just because you made a Vision Board and practiced affirmations.

It's also important that any reader who has experienced a pregnancy loss or loss through fertility treatments does not think that they could have prevented it with these methods or that they are at fault for their outcome.

As I go through the grief and search for my own "whys," I cannot help but question everything I have done or didn't do. Did I put too many things on my Vision Board and scatter my energy out too far? Was I focused too much on my book and what will manifest first? Was I too stressed about my husband's upcoming career change and a possible location change that I threw off the energy? Does the world feel like too dark of a place to incarnate right now? Did I do something Karmically that caused me to deserve this?

These are a few of the questions that I will not have the answers to in this lifetime. As the days go on, I will see more clearly the direction I am meant to go, and eventually what is supposed to happen. I do not feel that the door is completely closed on my having a second child, I may try again one day.

At least I was so lucky the first time and do have my wonderful daughter Ellee, that is very true. Times like these are when I restrain from saying "must be nice" the most. Because it must be nice for those who can conceive naturally and never had to think twice about fertility.

But I do not wish to say this to myself, it does not feel good inside of my body. Every pregnancy is a miracle and I choose to focus on that.

I am very blessed in several other ways, including the husband I have who truly loves me, and getting to call Hawai'i home. Having these things does not mean I deserve to struggle to conceive; nor does anyone else who may have the same.

Maybe the woman I envy for her ability to conceive naturally on social media has a husband who strays, or is miserable where she lives. In that sense I wouldn't choose her life over mine. In fact, I wouldn't choose to have anyone else's life over mine. I accept my life's journey as it is and work to co-create it as beautifully as I can.

My losses are as equal as my gains in that they are mine and part of my story. I choose to share my story in hope that it resonates with another and possibly guides them along their path. I do not wish to install false hope that everything will turn out exactly as you envisioned. We are working alongside the Universe and there are paths for us that we cannot see. We must continue walking no matter how uncomfortable it is.

The tools I've shared in this book are what help me to keep going with courage, strength, and ownership of my lessons. There may be times that things manifest with ease and grace, and others may require a few pit stops before they come to fruition. Some things we want may never manifest at all.

In the first hours I lost faith in my beliefs. I even thought, "How can I publish a book about manifestation when this happened?" I wondered what it all meant. But I believe in the work I have done so far, and have experienced success with the tools I provide throughout the chapters.

Although I experienced this devastating loss of my embryos, I did affirm, "I am pregnant when the timing is right."

Perhaps the timing is not right now. Having the embryos test abnormal prevented me from a miscarriage when I did transfer, which is another heartache I just wouldn't want to bear.

Slowly, the silver lining will reveal itself. I am grateful that I have two very different experiences to share with you. I do believe this was very important.

Please continue working towards your dreams and believing you deserve to live the life that you desire. I hope my personal story has been a source of inspiration and encourages you to remain strong on your journey. As I believe, you will not be given more than you can handle.

About the Author

Emilee J. Kern resides with her husband and daughter in Maui, Hawai'i. She is a 200hr RYT, 500hr CYT, Vision Board Workshop Facilitator, Law of Attraction Coach Practitioner, and completed her Health Coach Certificate in 2017 from the Institute for Integrative Nutrition. She studied oracle cards under Doreen Virtue, and became a Certified Angel Card Reader while living in Switzerland in 2014.

Inspired by her long-time usage of oracle cards, she has created the *Monarch Manifestor Oracle Cards* and guidebook that accompany the teachings throughout this book.

She considers herself an advocate for personal empowerment and shares her story in hope of being a source of encouragement to others on their own healing journey.

Website: www.emileejkern.com
IG @Emileejkern

Acknowledgments

I want to thank my publisher and editing advisor, Sylvana C. Candela. She was the shop owner I met while living in Colorado, from whom I purchased flower essences to aid me during my first IVF cycle. I reached out to her hoping to buy more essences for my second round of fertility treatments, and she told me she had just begun a publishing company. I had just finished my manuscript and hoped to meet the right person to help me publish it. It was divine timing, and I would like to thank her for her kindhearted spirit and support throughout the process. She was the first person to say, "You are an author." These are words I have longed to hear for a very long time. Sylvana and Peaceful World Publishing introduced me to her skilled team in the editing and publishing world.

I want to thank Wendy C. Garfinkle (Grammar Goddess Editing) for the thorough editing and professional interior formatting work. I appreciate you making yourself available to answer my inquiries, and quickly making additional edits as they arose.

Thank you, Taylor Dawn (Sweet 15 Designs), for going above and beyond what I could have envisioned myself for the cover design. You've taken the artwork and used your expertise to create a stunning and eye-catching design.

I want to thank my cover artist, Jessica Millman (Jessica Millman Tattoos), who has also been my tattoo artist. I have been infatuated with her talent for years, and have always envisioned her art partnered with my writing. The cover image came to me in a dream, and she was able to bring the vision to reality beautifully and with such realistic detail.

I want to thank Marquita Goodluck, an Udemy instructor whose course I took on "How to Write a Self-help Book That Heals." At first, I thought I had chosen the wrong course, but I realized that the program was precisely what I had been waiting for. My book had been an idea for years, and I never wrote a single page because I did not know where to start. Your coursework gave me the insight I needed to get it started.

I want to thank Tsuyoshi Artman, the artist of my *Monarch Manifestor Oracle Cards*. We met years ago on the farm on the Big Island, and after seeing his art on Instagram, I knew that his work was what I had been hoping for when designing my cards. Although his art is not in this book, his commitment to my vision gave me the encouragement and accountability for completing both my book and the oracle cards.

Thank you to my dear husband Beni, for being my biggest cheerleader. Your unwavering love and support for me and my dreams will never go unnoticed. Thanks for keeping our baby girl Ellee busy so I could get this project completed.

Thank you to all my friends and family who gave me advice on content, titles, and images. I appreciate the collective support in making this dream a reality.

Made in the USA
Monee, IL
22 April 2023

32264267R00072